MAYBE WE'LL HAVE YOU BACK

MAYBE WE'LL HAVE YOU BACK

THE LIFE OF A PERENNIAL TV GUEST STAR

Fred Stoller

Foreword by Ray Romano

Skyhorse Publishing

Skyhorse Publishing books may be purchased in bulk at special discounts for sales promotion, corporate gifts, fund-raising, or educational purposes. Special editions can also be created to specifications. For details, contact the Special Sales Department, Skyhorse Publishing, 307 West 36th Street, 11th Floor, New York, NY 10018 or info@skyhorsepublishing.com.

www.skyhorsepublishing.com

10 9 8 7 6 5 4 3 2 1

Library of Congress Cataloging-in-Publication Data is available on file.

ISBN: 978-1-62087-706-7

Printed in the United States of America.

CONTENTS

Foreword by Ray Romano ... vii

"You've Been on Everything!" ... 1

The Making of a Guest Star ... 9

"You're Too Depressed to Be a Comedian" ... 17

Welcome to L.A. ... 31

The Craft ... 35

Auditions ... 39

Worst First ... 45

Other People's Homes ... 55

Amen to Great Food! ... 57

Murphy Brown ... 63

Vinnie & Bobby ... 71

Can I Get Myself Hired as a Regular? "I Don't Think So" ... 75

An Empty Nest Is Better Than No Nest ... 81

Murphy/Clark ... 87

Don't Make Trouble ... 93

My *Seinfeld* Daze 97
Where I Left Off, but 20 Pounds Heavier 127
Can't Hurry Clones 131
Maximum Guest Star Exposure 133
Seinfeld Aftermath 139
The Breakout Film that Almost Broke Me 147
Kramer Reality 153
My Nanny Emmy 161
Suddenly Gay 165
Why Doesn't Raymond Love Me? 173
Some Friends 179
Norm Stole My Jacket 185
My Real Good Demo Reel 189
Looking for My TV Dharma 195
I Ain't No Scrub 203
The King Rules 211
The Quentin Tarantino Delusion 215
Tween Star 219
A Handy Gig 223
Building My Own Home 229
Life Imitating Art 235
My Awesome Showbiz Perks 239
Am I Somebody Yet? 245
A Roomful Of Weirdos 247
Being A Leading Man 249
Home 257
Acknowledgments 261

Foreword by Ray Romano

I first met Fred Stoller when I was starting to work as a stand-up in New York. I was never really aware of any physical similarity between him and me until I heard a club owner describe me as "What's his name, the healthy-looking Fred Stoller." You know what, I'll take it.

Fred had such a unique comedic style on stage. He was a regular at all the New York clubs. Every time I saw him, he made me laugh. Soon after I had met him, he moved out to Hollywood. It wasn't till years later that our paths crossed again. It was in the early stages of *Everybody Loves Raymond* when the producers and I decided to take advantage of Fred's comedic talent and similar look and cast him as my annoying cousin, Gerard. He killed it every time. Every line he muttered got big laughs. Without fail he always "brought the funny." He was just a great addition to the show. Also, the fact that he was on so many other shows fascinated me. I would constantly corner him and bug him with questions: "What's Seinfeld like?" "Is our food better than on the other shows?" "Does my pulse seem rapid?" He was a good barometer.

Truthfully, he was so good on so many shows before and after *Raymond*. How he hasn't gotten his own show is beyond me. But then I guess we wouldn't have gotten this hilarious, honest look at the world of a working actor.

Maybe We'll Have You Back gives the reader an opportunity to see this so-called glamorous world of acting from a straightforward and very funny perspective. Not only does he take you backstage through so many sitcoms and describes what that's like from a seldom-heard perspective, but his childhood, dating stuff, and in general, difficulty of fitting in are also fascinating and hysterical. He covers it all, from the women he dated (who only know you from your IMDb page), to how it is to explain to your parents that as an actor in L.A. not having to get a day job is in itself a huge victory. If you want an inside, funny, real look at the life of a hardworking actor, Fred Stoller is the perfect person to tell that story.

To be honest, I have a new show I'm writing and was thinking of making him a regular, but his voice as the outsider guy is so refreshing, why would I want to spoil that?

1

"YOU'VE BEEN ON EVERYTHING!"

I am on the set of *Friends*, nervously reciting my six lines in my head, waiting for David Schwimmer, who is directing the episode, to say "Action." For the second time in four seasons I am playing a dopey waiter who works in the kitchen alongside Monica, played by Courteney Cox.

When I get my cue, I walk toward the counter where she is preparing her food, trying hard not to look down for the little piece of tape that marks the exact spot I am supposed to stop at. I also have to make sure two extras who are playing waiters pass me before I deliver my first line. Little things, but as a guest star actor on a show as big as *Friends*, I don't want to make any mistakes.

"So, tonight's the night of the big bachelor party?" I ask her.

"Yeah! Hey! Thanks for getting me that girl's number."

"No problem. So who's the party for?"

"My husband."

"You hired your husband a hooker?" I hear my first few laughs and begin to loosen up.

"She's a stripper," Monica says, a bit concerned.

"No, she's a hooker," I bluntly reply, getting a few more laughs.

"Is that what they call strippers sometimes?" More laughs, our scene is clicking.

"When they're hookers," I answer.

"Oh my God Stu! I can't believe you did this! Now are you absolutely sure she's a hooker?"

"Either that or she's just the best, most expensive date I ever had."

Bingo! The live audience roars as Monica runs out to fix the mess I have gotten her into.

We nail the scene in only two takes, and just like that my job is done. Schwimmer tells me I did well, and to unwind from my momentary high I head off to munch on the snacks at the craft service table. As I down some free dumplings and sushi, Matt LeBlanc (Joey) starts rummaging through pizza boxes, trying to find a slice with his favorite toppings.

"The craft service woman here is really nice," I tell Matt. "I worked on *Dharma & Greg* a few weeks ago and the woman on that show was very nasty."

LeBlanc looks at me with utter amazement. "Man, you've been on every show. What show have you not been on? It's unbelievable!"

"Well, they're just these little guest star spots," I say.

He shakes his head in wonderment. "Man, I've seen you everywhere."

On the one hand, he was right. Since my first small role on the short-lived *Singer & Sons* in 1990, I have done more than sixty sitcom guest star appearances. When people stop me on the street and insist I list my credits so I can tell them where they know me from, most notably it's as the dim guy on *Seinfeld* who Elaine was attracted to only because he couldn't remember her, or Ray's annoying cousin on *Everybody Loves Raymond*, or the officious security guard on *Murphy Brown*, or the moronic pharmacist on

The Nanny, or perhaps as the role I was playing on *Friends*, the jerky waiter. Once in a while it might even be from some smaller hit I've been on, like the man attending the masochist's convention on *Wings*, the guy who was scared of losing his gallbladder on *Scrubs*, or the demented bellhop on *The Wizards of Waverly Place*. And there are some shows I've guested on no one knows about (*Living in Captivity*, *Can't Hurry Love*, *Alright Already*). I've played dozens of characters who are "offbeat," "annoying," "pathetic," and "depressed," all after years of establishing myself as a stand-up comedian whose persona is, well, kind of offbeat and depressed.

But as LeBlanc heads off, I am tempted to tell him that all the guest star appearances I'd made, and even writing for a season on *Seinfeld,* don't add up to half of one week's worth of his salary.

At the end of the *Friends* taping, it is curtain call time and there's always a very festive atmosphere on every set. They're either blasting the theme music of the show or some other high-energy crowd pleaser. Every show, from *Friends* on down to a lowly pilot that may never air, ends in this upbeat party atmosphere.

I get herded to the exact spot I have to be, based on the age-old pecking order of least significant to most significant role. Going before me is an actor that had one line as a waiter and the actress that portrayed the hooker.

I come out, get a polite round of applause and step aside for the other guests and the actual stars of the show, who come out to a thunderous ovation.

I used to think if I got a big enough round of applause, the producers would note this and make an extra urgent attempt to bring me back. But after so many curtain calls, I have come to realize that even if I got the four-minute ovation Michael Jordan got his last game before his third and final retirement, it still wouldn't matter.

Since I am one of the first, I get pushed all the way to the side, but I have to keep clapping for everyone who comes out after me. The *Friends* curtain call is a little different than other shows. No one cast member is more promoted than any other, so when the regulars start coming out, there is no ascension of applause, like on *Everybody Loves Raymond.*

We stand there, still clapping away, while the audience cheers and applauds. I am sort of happy. I am smiling, and I am feeling good, and I am a part of show business. But my claps start to feel hollow, my smile frozen. I know this cheerful party is going to end real soon. I am almost clapping to drown out the scary thoughts in my head about what lies ahead.

Curtain calls are very bittersweet for me. They mean it's the end of my treasured workweek, and I'm minutes away from going back to unemployment and uncertainty. The next day I'd be back on the meat market, going on cattle call auditions for parts I know I am wrong for. It could be months before the next gig.

Now the energy is fading: The music suddenly stops. The six stars head off, and the crowd gets up to leave. It's over. But I linger just a bit, pining for just a little bit more validation to keep me going. The executive producers of the show, Kevin Bright, David Crane, and Marta Kauffman, are going through the cast to say thanks, but get stopped and don't seem to be making their way all the way down the line to me. So I decide to go over and genuinely thank them for a fun week of work. I patiently wait for a pause in the conversation they're having with a network executive, fantasizing about those five words I hope to hear after every guest star spot I do: "MAYBE WE'LL HAVE YOU BACK."

It's the goal of every actor in my shoes who's had his six lines (sometimes more, often less) and tried to walk the fine line between not stealing the scene from the actual stars of a show but making enough of an impact that the audience, writers, critics, and viewers at home will remember me and want more.

Waiting for the showrunners I couldn't help but fantasize. Maybe this could be the time they tell me I am so funny, they had already devised stories to have me back and become an integral part of the show. Maybe I could be promoted to Monica's annoying boss and then it turns out we live in the same building and she can't get away from me. Or maybe, just maybe, they're thinking of giving Monica her own spin-off series about a restaurant, and I'll be the co-star.

But when I finally reach writer-producer David Crane, all I get is a big warm smile and a "Great job, Fred."

I'm not crushed or surprised. But the only way to go home happy is to keep hope alive in the back of my mind: surely having to do twenty-two plot lines a year, at some point they will need to bring back the memorably jerky, annoying waiter.

It's not the kind of career most people think of when they decide they want to be actors. And it's not the kind of career I expected when I started. But hey, it's a living. In what other profession could I profit from being nervous and nebbishy?

What's scary is how naturally these off-kilter parts come to me. On several auditions, directors have said to me, "Don't be so pathetic," when I had no idea I was being that. On more than one occasion, a show's wardrobe person has said, "Okay, you're playing the annoying, nervous guy," looked at their racks of possible choices and then back at me and asked, "Could we use your own clothes? The way you are is perfect for the character."

My knack for knowing how to dress like myself has an economic benefit: it entitles me to collect the union's mandatory wardrobe fee. The first time this happened, I worried that I was costing the producers more money, but then I found out this fee was $11. I don't know how they came up with the number eleven, but I'm sure negotiating that issue is what kept the entertainment industry shut down during the last brutal Screen Actors Guild strike. Now, whenever someone makes some snide comment to me that I don't dress cool, I reply, "Thirty-three bucks it's earned me, baby! Thirty-three bucks and counting!"

Getting cast on these shows is always a thrill, but I'm never around long enough to truly revel in it. Partly it's because I'm not the kind of guy who gets cast as a genuine love interest for a main character. If I am connected romantically, it's usually as a joke.

For me, being asked back isn't a pipe dream. It has happened several times, including *The Nanny* (four times over four seasons), *Murphy Brown* (five times over six seasons), *Everybody Loves Raymond* (six times in six seasons), and *Suddenly Susan* (five times in two seasons).

But my longest consecutive stint was back in 1992 when I worked five weeks in a row on the little known show *Vinnie & Bobby*. That show starred a pre-*Friends* Matt LeBlanc in the role of Vinnie.

I'm well aware that not every actor can be Matt LeBlanc. To be out of work is to be in quite a massive company. In the Screen Actors Guild, 90 percent of the active members are out of work at any given time and 10 percent work for less than eight weeks a year. I consider myself lucky for the work that I've had. In baseball analogies, I've had lots of singles, but never hit that big home run.

To outsiders, not to mention most fellow comedians and actors, it looks like I've got it made. My credits are several pages long and every so often I get diminishing checks in the mail when my episodes are rerun. I'm thrilled to be working in a union where only 2 percent of the members work.

I have had some years where I have only worked once or twice. I am lucky (mostly in the last fifteen years) to have stayed afloat, but am still looking for that one situation that sticks, that one good working environment that will shelter me from the humiliation and rejection of auditioning or from the despair of not having any auditions at all. I'm trapped in a weird kind of showbiz sitcom purgatory—I get enough work not to quit, but never enough to feel I can take a deep breath and stop struggling.

But, more than in almost any other profession, steady employment is hard to come by. After being around awhile I realized it's completely out of my control. No matter how hilarious my guest spot is, I'm just servicing the show, and there's a whole family of regular cast members, who have expensive contracts and story lines mapped out for them. So, now after I do a show, I try to forget about it and not worry whether the producers will bring me back. I try to relax, but I never do.

Being a perennial guest star is like being a foster kid being passed around some really great foster homes. I would love for one of them to keep me, but it's a hell of a lot better than being abandoned.

It only began to dawn on me that I had a story to tell when I was trying to live through a horrible date, at which my patchy career and life were put under uncomfortable scrutiny. We weren't really having any fun, and I couldn't figure out why she had even agreed to go out with me, until she started her litany of questions.

"According to IMDb you've been on many different TV shows."

I was weirded out. Sure, everyone researches prospective dates on the Internet—I've done it myself—but why was she broadcasting the fact?

"I saw you worked on *The Nanny*," she continued. "Was Fran Drescher difficult to work with? I have heard that about her."

I told her that Fran Drescher was very nice and tried to shift the conversation onto other things. Instead, she went right back to her research, as if I were an interview assignment. I don't usually mind questions, but she was asking them in a clinical way. To her, I was just a private Learning Annex seminar on the sitcom guest star life. Her course was free and included the meal she was eating, a little too slowly for my comfort.

The topics I was asked to cover included: How do you become a guest star actor? How much money can someone make if he's never been a regular on a show but has been on a lot of them? And most importantly, what's it like to be near more interesting and famous people than myself? And of course, she wanted to know as much as possible about *Seinfeld*. Whether my answers were true or jokes, she just kept plowing ahead.

"On IMDb, I saw that in 1994 you wrote on *Seinfeld*. Why didn't you continue there?"

"I wasn't very good."

"You have so many credits. I saw about sixty. But are you famous?"

"I'm actually seven credits short of being famous."

But the Chinese restaurant interview still wasn't over. She proceeded to assault me with such a barrage of questions I no longer even had time to answer.

"So, is this where you want to be in your career?"

"Why didn't you pursue the writing? Can't you make more money from that?"

"What TV show was your favorite to be on?"

"How'd you get into this?"

"Why weren't you on *Raymond* more than you were?"

"Were you always funny? You don't seem that funny now."

"Do you have a time limit before you give up on show business?"

Though I do have something of a masochistic streak when it comes to dating, even I have a time limit. So I got up, found the waitress and paid the check.

But a few days later, when surfing the net, memories of the date-interview spurred me to look up my page on IMDb (Internet Movie Database). There in chronological order were the seventy-plus appearances and my character names. I smiled as I recalled some of my favorite stops and cringed at some of the worst. There were a lot of stories to tell—and other stories that hadn't made it to the official résumé: the great parts I didn't get, the shows that never saw the light of day, all of the excruciating downtime, the tyrannical acting teachers, or all of the bizarre auditions. In a way, I started to understand why that woman had asked me all of those questions. I began wondering "How did I end up being this wandering TV actor?" And I realized when I stepped back from the daily anxiety that it's been an amazing and hilarious journey through many of the best and worst shows of the past twenty years.

2

THE MAKING OF A GUEST STAR

It isn't hard to figure out how I ended up with a career as TV's go-to schnook; it's a role I was born to play. Looks-wise, I was always a stick figure. Even when I stopped growing at 6'1" I still weighed only 130 pounds. Picture a skinnier Jughead, only with *no* confidence. Anytime anyone passed me, I always flinched like I was going to get hit. Throughout my life people have had loads of fun raising their hand in the air to see me flinch—including my demented math tutor and a TV repairman. I was so shy I could barely make eye contact with a cat, or a photograph.

I loved TV and movies, but the world of show business was galaxies away from mine. I thought to be on TV you had to start real young, like the kids from *The Brady Bunch*. I envied these actors. I'd see the cast of *Welcome Back, Kotter* or *The Partridge Family* having fun and kidding around with each other on talk shows and *Battle of the Network Stars*. They seemed like they were a part of something important together and I wanted to have that too.

Truth is, I wasn't brought up to dream big. I was raised in Sheepshead Bay, Brooklyn, New York, in a lower-middle-class Jewish neighborhood that consisted of rows and rows of identical two-family houses. On more than one occasion we'd hear drunken neighbors trying to insert keys into our door, thinking it was their home. The neighborhood was reminiscent of the one in *Saturday Night Fever*. I remember when the film came out that instead of everyone seeing how racist and small-minded it made them all seem, they strived to emulate the strutting, goombah-type it depicted, seeing it not as an indictment but as something to aspire to.

Growing up, there weren't a lot of expectations for me to excel in life, especially from my mother who was constantly panicked, like a hooked fish flapping around on the dock. All I heard from her my whole life was: "It's almost over," which would often be followed up with: "What do I have left, fifteen, twenty years? It's almost over!"

I'm pretty sure I'm the only nine-year-old who set up a lemonade stand and his mother reacted by panicking: "What if it goes under? Don't do it, Freddie."

She also panicked about my imminent rejection when I wanted to work at Burger King to earn my own spending money. "Yeah, right! Like they're waiting for you!" she brutally informed me.

My mother never gave me any responsibilities. She wouldn't even let me walk the dog, but then she'd make me feel guilty that my father was certainly going to have a massive heart attack for walking Bon-Bon, our neurotic French Poodle, in the cold. So once, when I was about twelve, I insisted that I walk Bon-Bon, but she blocked me at the door, yelling, "No, you don't know how! It's too hard for you."

My one sibling Cindy, who's six years older, was so detached from my parents that she never could bring herself to call them Mom and Dad; they were always Pearl and Morris. Cindy recently gave me her thoughts on why Pearl had such low expectations of me, but not of her. She theorized that since she did so well in school, Pearl figured, what was the chance that someone could have *two* children that were okay? "There has to be something wrong with one of them. I mean, what are the odds?" It was as if my mother had made up her mind before I was born that there'd be something defective with me.

I grew up petrified about my future. I had no faith that I had the necessary skills to become a grown-up with a daily job. My father's life did not inspire confidence. He was a commercial artist who designed displays for department stores and each day he'd spend almost two hours in rush hour traffic driving to work from the outskirts of Brooklyn to Manhattan and back. He'd always come home and sit two feet away from the TV with a martini in his hand. But, for some reason, he never sat facing the TV. He always sat parallel to it. It looked to me like he was going to have a drag race with the set.

My father never talked. He was able to. He wasn't mute, but he hardly spoke more than two sentences in a row. When my mother would go hysterical, my father would just withdraw by pretending he was reading. One time he just stared at a blank calendar for about fifteen minutes. Another time, I swear he spent ten minutes reading a matchbook cover. My mother, on the other hand, talked and screamed more than enough for both of them. I'd tell her I was going to Coney Island and she'd scream "It's so rough there! You'll come home in a box! Morris, say something! Say something to him!"

For the longest time I took her words literally and really believed that if you were murdered, they'd bring you back home in a coffin. I then wondered, if your parents weren't home, would they leave you by the door waiting for them to return?

Truth is, I favored the non-entity of my father over the constant noise of my mother. The most I ever saw him stand up to my mother was one night when my family was walking home after seeing the movie, *Charly*, about a mentally challenged man who is only briefly cured with an experimental drug. We stopped at a newsstand so my parents could buy the Sunday *New York*

Times. (I've never understood why the Sunday *Times* kept coming out earlier and earlier on a Saturday night.) But anyway, we waited on line and, for some reason, I was handed the big, bulky paper. And then, for some reason, I dropped it. It didn't fall apart or anything disastrous. But as the paper hit the ground my mother screamed at me, "You're just like Charly!" I saw my father flinch and his face scrunched in distaste at my mother's comment. This was the best stance I'd seen from him, and as inconsequential as it seemed, I appreciated it.

It's unfortunate I never had the over-compensating "*I'll show them! I can do anything in the world!*" instinct. Instead, I just bought into all of my mother's fears and self-doubt. She resented pushy, nervy people, and later admitted it was because she secretly wished she could be more pushy and nervy. I may have inherited that same disdain/envy for the annoying pushy go-getters.

I don't mean this to be an indictment of my mother. She tried her best, but she was saddled with many worries that she passed onto me with the highest anxiety. There were some incidents of generosity and support that I did appreciate. I feel it's only fair I mention some of those. Although she put up a fight, I did get to keep up with the fad of high-end sneakers my peers were buying. It must have been hard for her to understand. I was part of the generation that had that sudden expensive jump from regular Converse sneakers to $40 Walt Frazier Puma Clydes.

And she had a jovial side. It might have been something that tickled her that she displaced on me, but anytime a monkey came on TV, she'd scream for me to watch it and laugh hysterically how much the monkey amused me, even though I don't remember loving the monkey as much as she did. And she stuck up for me when I was literally left out in the cold. One day, when I was around fifteen, I came home from school and realized I'd forgotten my key. It was winter and I'd also forgotten my gloves. I headed down the street thinking my friend Hal would be home and we could hang out until my mother returned. Hal's mother opened the door and told me Hal wasn't there. "Okay, can I hang out in his room till he gets back?" I asked.

"No," she answered without a thought and closed the door.

I walked home and paced in front of my house, trying to keep warm. When my mother got back, she was livid when I told her Hal's mother wouldn't let me wait there.

"How could she do that?" my mother inquired. I was shocked when she marched herself down the street to Hal's house. She returned some time later, almost in tears, admitting she didn't have the courage to confront Hal's mother. "It's better to just let it go," she sighed, then showed me the book on assertiveness she'd checked out from the library, hoping in the future to do better at speaking up for herself.

What my mother wasn't shy about, however, was seeking out therapists for me. I went to see various ones since I was thirteen. One would tell racist jokes and get mad at me for being uptight and not laughing at them. And then for a brief while, she began seeing her own therapist. She'd come back from a session and for an hour or so be very nice: "How was your day, Freddie?" "Are you excited about any TV shows on tonight?" "I brought you some cookies." I have to say that scared me to death.

I knew the shrink must've instructed her to make an extra effort to be nice to me, and I have to give her credit that she was trying her hardest, but I also knew that smile on her face would wear off rather soon and things would just go back to the way they always were. After a few months she announced she was quitting therapy. "I know I have hang-ups. You go! You deal with it!" So I went. After three sessions she said, "So, are you better yet?"

Out of all my mother's neuroses, I think she was most afraid of me not doing well in school. She had been left back in first grade because she'd been very ill and had missed a lot of days. So I could never miss school, no matter how sick I was. I could be gushing blood and she'd say, "School goes on whether you're there or not!" For years in a row, I won a perfect attendance certificate. Other kids may have been good at sports or drawing or music, but my greatest accomplishment was sticking my arm up in the air and calling, "Present!"

My mother also insisted I have a regular tutor, and I later found out that she paid others to secretly tutor me. She gave my babysitter, my sister's friends, and some kids on the street small amounts of money to sneak in math lessons in any unsuspecting way they could. Most of them, though, had no math skills and just pocketed the cash.

Although I had that impeccable attendance record, I still felt invisible in school. I only had the one friend, Hal, who lived down the street (and who, to this day, still lives down the street, with his unwelcoming mother). I was often jealous of the kid in my class who always got chased and beaten up. I could never figure out why he was the chosen one; he wasn't chubby or brainy or anything that distinctive. But then one day when he was absent, they chose me to pick on; they chased me and pulled my string tie through the fence and threw me down. It was actually kind of thrilling. For once, I wasn't invisible. The next day, when the other kid returned, I felt a little sad it was over.

Let's just say my imagination was not exactly encouraged. My mother threw out my G.I. Joe action figures because she thought I was a sissy for playing with "dolls," so I resorted to clothespins to enact my mock battles.

To escape the fear I had about the world out there, I had two outlets. First was my imaginary basketball league. I'd shove a wire coat hanger I rolled into the shape of a hoop into the opening at the top of my bedroom door and closed it so it stayed in its place. My ball was a rolled up pair of socks. For hours on end I played games. But the basketball stars I grew up with such as Willis Reed, Dave DeBusschere, and Walt Frazier didn't play in my bedroom. The players I invented had names, faces, and skills totally unlike anyone I had ever seen. There was Globolo, the tall thin guy with just one arm. And Dvest, the short muscular black guy who'd probably be labeled autistic today. He didn't speak or communicate. One had a facial deformity, one shook nervously, one swatted the ball like a volleyball, and the rest were other misfits who shined in my bedroom.

My other outlet was acting out scenes from my favorite movies. But unlike most kids who grow up idolizing decisive, macho heroes like Clint Eastwood or Harrison Ford, I shunned the stars and gravitated toward the invisible bit players or outcast characters. In *Dog Day Afternoon*, I pretended I was the guy who chickened out in the beginning. In *The Parallax View*, I was the guy with the tuba who points out the bad guy. On long car rides I'd sit in the backseat with my head pressed against the window pretending I was Ratso Rizzo from *Midnight Cowboy* on his doomed bus ride to Florida. And I'd spend hours pretending to be Billy, the mentally disabled deaf mute from *The Last Picture Show*, who spends the whole movie sweeping only to get killed by a truck. I'd sweep the house with an imaginary broom and then lie on the floor, face down, pretending I too was run over by a truck. A less disturbing hero was Donald Sutherland playing the goofy character amongst all the other macho stars in *The Dirty Dozen*. I also connected with guys like Herb Edelman and Ron Leibman, and any other quirky character actor who made me sit up in my seat like a lone dog when it sees another of its own species. "I could do that! I could be that!" I'd exclaim. I knew I had no hope of being the leading man, but I could be an awkward blind date; I could trip and crash into the wedding cake.

Then, when I was in high school, I discovered another way you could get on TV, even if you didn't start as a kid. One night, I tagged along with my sister and her friends to Pips, a local Brooklyn comedy club. Somehow I got in without being carded. Richard Lewis and Billy Crystal were performing; neither had broken through yet. Crystal actually did a bit about fake IDs. He said, "I see we have some people that snuck in tonight." Despite being terrified that I was going to be singled out for being underage, I remember laughing. More than that, I became mesmerized with the idea of being a comedian. I had seen comics on *The Ed*

Sullivan Show and *The Tonight Show*, but seeing it live and up close made it seem so much more accessible.

Even though Crystal wasn't famous yet, he had a life from just doing comedy. That intrigued me. I had never been a big student of stand-up comedy, but I remember noticing on the back of the menu a list of all the famous comics that had started at that club: Rodney Dangerfield, David Brenner, George Carlin, Joan Rivers. One of my sister's friends told me that actors like Jimmie Walker from *Good Times* and Freddie Prinze from *Chico and The Man* did routines at a comedy club in Manhattan and were spotted for *The Tonight Show*. From that, they got to be on a TV show. Even though both Walker and Prinze would end up as subjects on the *E! True Hollywood Story*, back then they were gods to me. The idea of *me* putting an act together began gestating that night. For the first time in my life, I thought there could actually be a place in the world for a guy who so far had only been noticed for raising his arm in the air.

3

"YOU'RE TOO DEPRESSED TO BE A COMEDIAN"

It's kind of amazing that I made the decision to get onstage in front of strangers and tell jokes, since at seventeen I was so shy, I practically needed to ask permission to enter a supermarket.

It was the summer before I graduated high school and also my eighth year at Camp Sequoia, an eight-week sleep-away camp in Upstate New York where I had risen up the ranks to camp waiter. I bought the comedy albums of Richard Pryor, Steve Martin, and George Carlin to start off my research. For those eight weeks I honed my routine muttering my jokes to myself while walking alone in the woods. But then a bully went through my cubby and found my notebook I was using to craft my routine and read it aloud to everyone else.

"My name is Fred Stoller and if you never heard of that name before, you're deaf because I just said it."

"What kind of retard writes a letter to his parents and says what his name is?" he taunted.

I tried explaining it wasn't a letter, but a joke I was writing. "A joke? What kind of joke is that?"

I knew I couldn't tell all of them I wanted to be a comedian and get my dreams trampled on so early in the game. But I told myself that when summer was over, they'd be surprised that the guy they called "Galaxy Man" (because I always took off and went into my own world) would end up in a world of comedic stardom on game shows, talk shows, and movies!

When camp was over and I got back home, I went as soon as I could to The Improv, a famous New York comedy club where I was determined to make my mark. It hadn't occurred to me that before my first time stepping on stage, it would have been wise to visit different comedy clubs to get a feel for the place, the comics, and how tough the crowd may be. But who had time to think about scoping out clubs—I had TV stardom waiting for me! That Sunday night there were dozens of other hopefuls like me who had waited hours on line praying that they could pass the audition. "Passing" meant the right to hang out all night in the bar so that maybe once every few weeks you'd get a shot to perform for no money very late at night after most of the crowd had gone home. On line was a guy actually skinnier than me named Steven Buse. His act consisted of him taking his shirt off and making muscles. I'd later see him pop up in movies when he went back to his real name, Steve Buscemi.

That first audition, I talked so fast that my five-minute prepared routine took only about three minutes. My jokes were not sophisticated, I talked about pay toilets. I said, "They should make it that you have to pay to get out, because anyone would pay to get out of there with that smell." I also did one about asking this girl out. She told me I had to gain weight. I told her that every time I look at her, I do gain weight. I didn't realize an erection meant you didn't actually gain weight, but your weight was just a bit distributed elsewhere.

One night, I did a little better than the others. On the train ride to the club, I came up with this routine and, with nothing to lose, tried it out. "My friend told me that he was at a party, and he ate so many cookies, 'it wasn't even funny.' Does that mean eating cookies is usually funny, but not in his case?" And then I took out some cookies and proceeded to eat them as I waited and got a few laughs. When I got off stage, another open mic comedian said, "You eating cookies, now that's funny. You did that funny."

But the long train rides to Manhattan for the longer waits to being rejected was more than I could take, so I quit and went to Kingsborough Community College as a way to keep my mother off my back. In some of my classes I sat with convicted felons. They were let out of prison to study at Kingsborough during the day and then had to report back at night. One fellow English student decided to skip school one day and go on his own field trip instead, a kidnapping and robbery spree at the local mall. He was sent back to a maximum security prison which he escaped from and went on another notorious kidnapping spree. He may well be Kingsborough's most renowned former student.

During college, I worked for several years at horrible part-time jobs. I sold bootleg T-shirts at rock concerts where I had to watch out for the cops or the hired security of the rock groups or other vendors who tried to pickpocket my earnings. At Coney Island amusement park, I worked at a cheap haunted house called "The Tunnel of Laughs." The ride was slow and dull, so to give the customers some sort of a fright, I was paid to dress up as the Wolfman and jump out and scare them. During several heat waves, I had to stand in the hot tunnel, wearing a heavy furry mask, waiting for the next car to pass. It got so hot that sometimes I'd take the mask off, put it on my fist, and just shoved it at the people. On several occasions, gang kids who were mad I scared them went on the ride again, knowing I was going to be there, and spit and swung at me. I'd sit in the tunnel between rides and think, "What the hell am I going to do with my life?" I felt as terrified about my future as when I was a kid. The Bruce Springsteen song "Factory" kept going through my head. It was just the working life for me, too.

Although three years had passed, I finally decided that I had to go back to the comedy clubs. I blocked out the prior rejections and recalled I did get those laughs when I ate those cookies. So

I walked out of the dark tunnel, handed the owner my Wolfman mask, and quit.

After my three-year absence, I felt I had a stronger resolve to make it happen this time. On August 6, 1978, I was twenty years old and number thirty-seven on line for The Improv. I finally got onstage at around one in the morning. Besides my new opening joke, I did probably the only "political" joke of my career: "I think Gerald Ford was going after the Italian vote. Yeah, he made over fifty vetoes." My big statement on religion was, "It's a waste. Look at the Jews, for example. When we want to pray, we often go to The Wailing Wall. What good does that do? It's like talking to a wall." And my big closing was the last impression I ever did in my career: Ed McMahon. McMahon, of course, was famous for saying "And, heeeeeere's Johnny!" My impression was of Ed McMahon as a baby, "Goo Gooooo, Ga Ga!"

Luckily, the few scattered audience members who remained happened to connect with me. Those jokes didn't last in my act for more than a month, but for some reason, that night they did the trick. Perhaps the audience appreciated my do-or-die determination to sell those jokes and start a new life. They were with me for every beat and gave me a big ovation when I left.

When I got offstage I passed the emcee, Robert Wuhl (who years later would end up being the star and creator of *Arli$$*), who told me to see the manager in the bar, Chris Albrecht. Albrecht,who ended up being the head of HBO, said that if I wanted to, I could start hanging out at the club. I was so excited; I didn't sleep for three days. I decided to quit college. I needed to spend all my time hanging out all night at The Improv, hoping they'd put me on.

My mother did not quite comprehend my career choice. "You're so depressed, how are you going to make people laugh?" And I have to admit I could understand her bafflement. No one had ever told me I was funny. None of my relatives knew me to talk more than my father did. I only had a few friends and none of them thought I was funny. I didn't even think I was funny. But somehow

I had gotten my foot in the door at The Improv and I saw that as a way to find my place in the world somehow.

My family ended up helping me develop my best material. They'd just open their mouths and all I had to do was repeat what they said verbatim:

"My mother's not very proud of me that I do this. She doesn't tell her friends that I'm a comedian. She tells them I'm retarded."

"My mother freaked out cause I quit college to do this. She's always saying 'you got to get your degree.' I say 'what for, what's it going to do for me?' This is her reason: She says, 'You'll be able to say you're a college graduate.' Like I'm not able to say it now? Like I try, 'I'm a cogger gradugate. I'm a coleberagabubate.' Damn, four credits short, I almost had it!"

"I asked my sister why my parents like her better than me. She said it's because she's older and they've known her longer."

The onstage persona that I was gradually developing reflected who I was as much as who I wasn't. I hardly had any life experience. I was still as socially adept as a battered timid kid who had awoken from a coma after twenty years. I didn't have enough self-esteem to be conversational so I'd just shoot out morbid non-sequitur one-liners with my head down, keeping my hands busy by making a noose with the microphone cord.

For a short while I opened by standing onstage for a few moments before stating, "I was killed in Vietnam." Other jokes were similarly cheerful.

"You people are going to see me on TV in a few years. And when you do, you'll be able to say, 'Wow, I saw that guy before he killed those eight people.'"

"My cousin killed himself because no one would play with him. He hung himself from a pole in his backyard. Now people play with him."

"I hate my guts."

"Last week I was on the ledge of a building, twenty stories up. Below me, a crowd of people formed, and they started yelling, 'Don't spit!'"

I remember the first time I was approached after delivering my stand-up routine. A very business-like woman came up to me and handed me her card. She told me that after seeing my act she had some ideas on how she could work with me. She said I should call her. I was so excited until I looked at her card and saw that she was a psychotherapist. A year after hanging out and vying for stage time, some peers were taking to my style and material. Some audience members understood that my jokes were jokes and not a cry for professional help.

In 1980, I was able to do the second scariest thing I had ever done, besides getting onstage my first time: I moved out of my parents' house. A friend had told me of an apartment in New York City for just $130 a month. It was actually more a room than an apartment. The bathroom and shower were in the hall and I had to share them with two other rooms up there on that fifth-floor walkup. But still, it was in Manhattan, and I could always get out! (Three years later I upgraded to another apartment where I had my own bathroom, but the shower was in a bathtub in the kitchen that was propped up four feet up in the air. To shower I had to climb a stepladder.)

I had several sources of income that helped me pay my rent during that time. I found a part-time job handing out tickets so people could preview and rate possible new CBS TV shows. I'd write my name on the back of each ticket and get a dollar for each tourist I could convince that sitting in a room watching a tape of a TV show they had never heard of would be a good time. Well, I didn't exactly sell it that way. I'd say they were seeing a free CBS TV show! If they'd ask, I'd fess up, but if they thought they were seeing *The Price Is Right*, or one of their other favorites, the better for me.

Sometimes there'd be fights between vendors for the prime territory at 47th and Broadway where tourists lined up for half-priced Broadway tickets. I had a partner, a big guy named Colin who was reminiscent of Lenny from *Of Mice and Men*. Colin would toss his bag of tickets down and lunge at any other vendors he claimed were in our great spot. I never watched any of the shows I handed out tickets for and I didn't quite know about the mechanics of the TV pilot I was fighting with other vendors to push at the time. Besides my CBS ticket job, I also actually started making money from stand-up comedy. The comedy boom of the eighties was just starting to explode. It enabled me to eke out a marginal living playing a dingy bar somewhere and then eating there for free. Most comics didn't even need representation. At the peak of the boom, all you had to do to get work was answer the phone. There were dates available for anyone with any semblance of an act.

Typically, three comics would meet at The Improv in Hell's Kitchen near the Lincoln Tunnel. The comic who owned a car would drive the other two out to some bar or disco in New Jersey. Weeknights, you could make $55 for a half-hour set. Many comics were able to get work solely based on the fact that they owned a car. Some even included that on their résumé.

Outside New York City, my act went over a fair amount, but too many times my low-key style wouldn't go over in the suburbs with the rowdy drunken patrons in their hometown bars. It seemed they'd much rather see some high-energy act run around the stage singing TV theme songs or insulting them in some way. So often, I'd bomb and then the act following me would blow the roof off the place. It would be too unbearable to hear them cheering him on after hating, or at best, mildly tolerating me, so I'd walk outside in the freezing cold or on a lonely deserted road to escape his adulation. And these acts would go on forever. One time after waiting an hour and a half for the headliner to end so he could drive me home, I then had to wait some more when the club turned back into a disco and he danced the night away with all his adoring fans.

I was never a die-hard "Let me slay this crowd!" comic who loved being on stage. It honestly never felt natural being up there for more than three minutes or so. And that had nothing to do with my act doing well or not. It just didn't suit the style of the quick-hit, depressive jokes I had to stretch out to fill up the time.

Most clubs flashed a light when your time was up. I loved getting the light. Once, I got in trouble for getting off too early, but it wasn't my fault. Apparently, this regular customer hated me and had his own flashlight. He stood in back and flashed it. All I saw was that wonderful light and I left the stage fifteen minutes too early. The manager was upset and forced me to get back onstage and resume. By that time though, most of the crowd had left.

Eventually, I was doing sometimes six sets on the weekends and sometimes even a couple during the week, which was enough work to quit my CBS ticket job, but I was stuck in something that I never intended to spend years and years doing. I was mistaken in thinking that doing my sometimes well-appreciated routine was going to get me to my real dreams. I didn't really have that compulsion to be up there every night in front of packed crowds. I wanted to be on a set, interacting with other people and not have the whole onus on me. I wanted to be in movies like Steve Martin or be on *Saturday Night Live* or some other hit TV show.

Once a year, the man who booked the comics for *The Tonight Show* would come to New York looking for fresh talent, but I was never one of those he got to see. *The Tonight Show* for awhile was the ultimate revered launching pad. I had seen Jerry Seinfeld, Bill Maher, and Larry Miller plucked out for their shots. A fellow CBS ticket vendor's brother was an aspiring West Coast manager. I called him up and he said he could set up a *Tonight Show* audition for me at The Hollywood Improv. So, I took what money I could spare and bought a plane ticket to Los Angeles. On the night of the showcase they put me on first, a terrible spot, because the crowd was still milling in and ordering drinks. If that wasn't bad enough, my contact was talking himself and his other clients up to the *Tonight Show* booker while I was trying to perform. Afterwards, I chided the manager for ruining my shot and flew home that same night.

On January 28, 1986, I was put in a very nerve-wracking situation that I thought would lead to my big break. With four hours' notice, the producers of *Late Night with David Letterman* called and asked if I would be available to be on the show that day. Apparently, they had had a cancellation. Getting called to make an appearance on such a big show at the last minute was obviously not the best situation. I wouldn't be listed in *TV Guide* and wouldn't have much time to prepare. But for where I was in my career, there was no way I could pass up on Letterman! Not being in *TV Guide*, I'd soon learn, was the least of the reasons why doing *Letterman* that day was not an ideal situation. My apartment had no TV reception and wasn't installed for cable, so I was oblivious to the fact that on that day America was recoiling in shock after the space shuttle *Challenger* exploded.

I rushed to the NBC studios in the legendary 30 Rockefeller Plaza and only then discovered why no one had wanted to do the show. I had to do my act for the producers in their office, where TV monitors replayed the horror over and over again. They had to make sure I didn't do any material that was inappropriate for that day. They didn't want me to do anything "too morbid." Unfortunately, that was half my act.

In his opening, Letterman apologized to the audience for doing the show. He said that he didn't mean to be irreverent on this tragic day in history, but they were going to try to do the show anyway. I was trying not to be selfish, but couldn't help thinking, *No one is going to watch the show. Who is going to laugh? This show will never be shown in reruns.*

I did sort of okay for the situation. It was obviously a sullen mood. Years later, I saw Letterman on *The Late Late Show* with Tom Snyder, and he said that the hardest show he ever had to do was the day the space shuttle blew up. At least he didn't say it was so hard because I was on it.

Months later, I performed several other five-minute bits for the *Letterman* producers, trying to get back on the show. By then, I had come out of my shell a little and was a bit more conversational and accessible. They said they wanted me to go back to when I was weirder. I tried, but many of those old jokes weren't working anymore. It felt like I was doing an imitation of what I used to be. But I was soon distracted from getting back on *Letterman* by some other opportunities.

Saturday Night Live is every comic's dream launching pad. The only thing standing in my way was Al Franken. Years before his fame as a best-selling author, Franken spent one season as the head producer of *Saturday Night Live*. A scout for the show thought my act seemed interesting and brought me in to audition for Franken. I did a few minutes of my act before he stopped me. He asked how I could be on the show. I was all excited, I thought I had the perfect way. "I'll be this cast member that does these characters that just miss. I do my best and I am not quite, let's say, an L.A. surfer dude or a French wine critic." I added that I wouldn't be doing the characters like all these other cast members, who know how to do dialects and all that stuff.

"So how would I use you? You're saying you'd be this guy that's always a little bit off? That's it?"

"Yeah, it would be great! You know, I'd do a character, but I'm not one of these guys that's going to look like them or know how to do all the mannerisms."

He said, "That's the second time you told me what you *can't* do." I sat there, stunned. All I could think was, did he have to put me down like that? Was he my father giving me life lessons? But he may actually have been right. As much as that stung, it did help. Now I try to only say what I can't do once during an interview, never twice.

Then came my David Brenner experience. Brenner was one of my favorite comedians. In 1986, he hosted a short-lived late night talk show called *Nightlife*. I got booked and my act went over very well. I mostly talked about my mother, how she always says the phrase "again." "Again with the TV on." "Again with the candy." She'd say it to anything. She'd come into my room at four-thirty in the morning and go, "Again with the sleeping. Again with the feet at the end of the legs."

But what I enjoyed the most was sitting down and interacting with Brenner on the panel. I talked about how exciting it was the time he had followed me at the comedy club Catch a Rising Star. I had a good set and during our interview reminded him that he had said, "That kid is going to be a star, unless he gets hit by a truck."

"Yeah, I think I remember saying that," Brenner admitted.

"Well, the only problem is," I said, "last week I got hit by a truck."

After that show, I felt comfortable enough with Brenner and his staff to come by and say "hi" a few times. Dave Wilson was Brenner's director and had been the original director of *Saturday Night Live*. His son, Mike Wilson, was Brenner's talent coordinator. I put together a few sketches, thinking perhaps I could write for *Saturday Night Live*. I thought Mike Wilson would have a contact there. Instead, he gave my material to Bob Tischler, Brenner's executive producer.

Tischler called me up and said that my sketches were good and noted that their sensibility seemed to be based around my distinct persona. One sketch was about a timid guy who decides to do risky things, called "The Thrill Seeker." My Thrill Seeker would do dangerous things like step into a pool ten minutes after eating a tuna fish sandwich, or eat an apple at a deli without washing it first. Another bit was about a guy who volunteers to be a Big Brother. There is a mix-up and he is matched with another guy like him who wants to be a Big Brother. They each think that the other is the little brother and they take each other on rides and play tag.

Tischler then offered me a staff job on *Nightlife* where I'd come up with little walk-on bits for myself, like what Chris Elliott did on *Letterman*.

At first, it was amazing. I had my own office! Sure, it was a little room that never would have passed an electrical safety inspection, there were exposed wires and twisted pipes all the way to its high ceiling. But that didn't matter. I had a steady salary and a break from vying for stage time at the competitive clubs and Jersey bars and discos. I was earning about $800 a week, the most I had ever earned in my life.

My first piece they did was a corny little bit in Brenner's monologue. He did a set up for a joke. "Yesterday it was so cold..." He waited until he got the standard Carson-like, "How cold was it?" response from the audience. He said, "Ever wonder why audiences scream that out? I'm going to show you a showbiz secret." And in the mode of an applause sign, they showed instead a flashing sign that prompted the audience to scream out, "How cold was it?"

But the most exciting moments of my life were the bits that they hired me to perform. First, we filmed the "Thrill Seeker" video. It was a minute routine in which, wearing a silly jumpsuit and a crash helmet, I stepped onto an escalator and bravely raised my arms in the air. Then, I entered a bar after I had counted that it had exceeded the safe occupancy limit. And on panel, I did more Thrill Seeker jokes that would end up becoming a mainstay in my stand-up act: "I did the *TV Guide* crossword puzzle with a pen!"

Once, I actually took bandleader Billy Preston's place and sang the theme song to the show. Later in the bit, Billy crawled out from the side of the stage where it was revealed that I had him tied up. And once, while playing an usher, I interrupted Brenner's monologue by crossing in front of him and seating a few people coming in late to the show.

Performing on the show was thrilling. For the first time, I felt closest to what I was about in my showbiz career. I felt my persona was utilized the best in these quirky situations that I had created. One day, Mike Wilson came into my office and told me that his father had worked on *Saturday Night Live* with John Belushi, Steve Martin, and Bill Murray and said that I had that special something those actors had. I was psyched. When Wilson left my office, I remember popping in a tape of Peter Gabriel's song "Big Time" and singing along, jazzed that I, too, was on the way to making it big time.

The only problem was what was going on behind the scenes. I was about to learn the basic showbiz lesson that everyone's first priority is rarely about making the best show possible, but rather advancing themselves.

Working on the show was also the first job for this scared little twenty-four-year-old redheaded writer. He had made up this point system he was sure was used for determining if a writer would be kept or not. He said that a joke in the monologue was worth one point, a whole set bit was worth five, and if you came up with a bit that could be a recurring desk piece, that was worth twenty points. He also deducted points if jokes didn't work. This demented point system he devised probably contributed to a mood disorder he might already have had. Some days he'd bust into my office with the bravado of a high school student who had just slept with a movie star, bragging about how many points he had scored. And some days, he'd be wailing in the halls, quivering about how he was going to be fired. And he'd always fight about who came up with what jokes and who should get the points for them.

For me to pitch an idea, I had to go though the head writer, who was a burly, scruffy man who'd had a brief stint doing stand-up comedy in the San Francisco Bay area some years before. After my first few pieces with Brenner had gone over, whenever I told him I had an idea he'd harshly ask, "For who!? Who's it for? For you again? We need topical jokes. All your bits you pitch are for you." It made no sense. Even when I tried going directly to Tischler to pitch an idea, he too said, "Who's the idea for? For you?"

I was relegated to my office with stacks of newspapers, where I tried to be a team player and write topical jokes, but those jokes got trounced in the point system while the head writer green-lit a few bits he wrote that he got to perform. Very quickly, the show was in shambles. The ratings were horrible. There were rumors that Motown Productions (which produced it) wasn't happy with Brenner and were looking to replace him.

By then, my thirteen-week contract was up, and I was let go. Shortly after, the redheaded kid was let go, and soon the plug was pulled on the whole show.

But I did manage to use the status of being on Brenner's show to be one of several New Yorkers who signed that year with the venerable William Morris Agency. Someone I knew set up a meeting with an agent, who had seen my act at several of the comedy clubs. He said he might be able to get the other higher-level agents to approve me because I was on staff on Brenner's show. I didn't tell him that I had just been let go a few days earlier. One of their West Coast agents asked if I would be out there for pilot season because they'd be able to set me up on many auditions. Finally, I felt it was my time. After ten years in New York, I had the "in" I was looking for in Hollywood. I was ready for my big break. Perhaps soon some vendor would be handing out free preview tickets to one of *my* pilots.

4

WELCOME TO L.A.

Soon after I first moved to L.A., I found myself at the Improv comedy club being complimented by one of the stars who had inspired me. Billy Crystal was hanging out with a friend and remembered my act from seeing it years earlier in New York. Still scared about having made the big move West, I was amazed to hear Crystal telling his friend how funny I was. He asked if I was going to perform that night. I explained that I didn't have a spot, that getting stage time was very difficult in Hollywood. I was so excited that such a big talent was a fan of mine, I felt his support could perhaps turn into something very big. I knew he was good friends with Rob Reiner, the very successful film director. I felt I wasn't so out of line when I volunteered, "I have a demo tape. Can I give you that?"

Suddenly Crystal's whole mood shifted. "You pushed it," he said as he turned his head away from me. I sheepishly slunk away from him.

That experience was exactly the sort of novice mistake I dreaded—and was destined to make in those first few months after arriving in Hollywood. I couldn't help but be desperate and anxious.

The pressure of being a relocated actor in L.A. is enormous. In New York, no matter how dissatisfied I felt with my life or career, I always knew that there was the possibility of Hollywood up ahead. But once you actually move to Hollywood, it means you've finally broken the piggy bank of hope and exhausted all possible resources. If it doesn't work, where do you go? Some people put off that scary last stop as long as possible. When I finally made the move I was already thirty.

Getting stage time at the comedy clubs was a lot tougher than in New York. On any given night the likes of Jay Leno, Jerry Seinfeld, or Robin Williams would pop in and bump us unknowns off the show. My *Letterman* and Brenner credits really didn't mean much. Also, a lot of club owners became managers of comics, and if you weren't managed by one of them, it made it that much more difficult. I wasn't able to make a living on the outskirts of town like I did in New York, so to be able to afford to stay in L.A., I had to leave town and work on the road. William Morris did have a department for road work, but that agent never helped me that much. When I'd call and tell him I needed work he'd say, "Look, no one's knocking on your door."

"Well, isn't it your job to knock for me? Build me up? Tell them I've been on *Letterman* and cable?" I was trying to restrain myself from smashing my phone against the table with the frustration of the stupidity I was dealing with. I'd soon regret pushing him to earn his 10 percent and actually do some work. I'd work at comedy clubs across the country where crowds would stare at me sometimes as if to say, "I didn't know Hinckley escaped."

When you headline on the road, you need nearly an entire hour of material, and I quickly realized my style and cadence didn't lend itself to keeping an drunk audience's attention for an hour. The breaking point for me came at Laff's Comedy Club in Tucson. The job started off horribly when the club's cook, who was supposed to pick me up at the airport, forgot. The phone number of the club was 97-FUNNY, which made it all the more unsettling to be seething mad spelling out the word "funny" on the pay phone every ten minutes, badgering him to come get me. I was practically pushing the keys through the phone.

I already knew that my first show didn't go well. I didn't need the owner to show me all of the negative remarks from the patrons who'd been encouraged to voice their opinions on the comment cards at their tables. "Wasn't fast enough." "He sucked." "Didn't make me laugh and I hated him."

The worst part after bombing that first night was having to go back to the depressing "comedy condo." Like most comedy condos, it was in a section of town nowhere near walking distance to anything except perhaps a 7-Eleven. The club owners bought these condos so they didn't have to put the comedians up in a hotel. On only a few rare exceptions would the place be cleaned up from the comedian who had stayed there the week before. There were still food containers on the floor, dirty sheets on the bed, and in this case, even the comedian from the week before on the couch. He was a road comic with nowhere to go until his next gig and hoped I wouldn't mind if he crashed for another few days.

I shut myself in my room, let the pushy intruding comic have the couch and TV, and I vowed not to spend my career being a miserable comedian, getting vilified by club owners and humiliated by negative comment cards. Acting classes would be my way out! Becoming a committed trained actor would be my edge!

5

THE CRAFT

My first acting teacher had us read scenes while another student would shove us repeatedly. I wasn't quite sure of the point of that exercise. I found it peculiar but no one else in class seemed to question it and I was too intimidated by the teacher to ask why. Paul, the know-it-all doorman at the Improv comedy club had highly recommended him so I trusted that there must be a strong benefit to learning how to recite material without being tipped over.

The teacher was an ex-actor (no surprise) who was shamelessly trying to use his students to break into a writing career. Once, a student in my class announced he got a small guest role on *Saved by the Bell*. The teacher's chubby red face started twitching with nervous excitement as he got up and headed toward the student. "Tell them about me, will you? I got a really great idea for a show about a high school!"

After quitting that class, I hooked up with a teacher recommended by comedian Rob Schneider who would later be on *Saturday Night Live* (and give me a part as a reporter in his film *The Animal*). For $275 a month, about forty of us sat in the cramped bleachers while he pushed each student's personal buttons: "Sarah, you're overweight, not a beauty queen, and still alone. Use that torment in the scene!" When I hinted that I was going to quit the class, he suddenly began praising my progress.

He would assign each student a scene and another student to do the scene with him. Since these classes were stuffed to capacity, you would only do your scene maybe once a month, but according to the disciples in the class, it was just as fulfilling to watch the teacher give his brilliant notes to the others as it would be to actually go up and perform yourself.

We'd have to rehearse with our partner a few times a week outside of class, and if my partner was a woman, that usually was the high point of my social life. Just her showing up at my place, or me going to hers made me feel I was with someone, even for just a short while. I was even assigned a few scenes where kissing was involved. Looking back, I'm suspicious if that was another ploy to keep lonely people paying the big bucks for the classes.

Once I was with my partner in my apartment rehearsing a scene from *Annie Hall*. She was a nice-looking woman from Germany. At the end of the scene we were supposed to kiss. So we get to the end of the scene and she French kissed me. She initiated it, I swear! We continued to kiss for about thirty seconds. After that I kept rehearsing and rehearsing, talking faster than my usual droll self to get to the kissing. And each time, we would make out. Finally I had to say something. "Can we kiss without the scene?" She looked at me, horrified. "What!? I am married!" So I nodded, rehearsed the scene again, and made out some more at the end of it. Sounds like a good scam, but for all the years and money I put into class, it wasn't worth the cheap thrills. Not only was I taking a class, but I was also shelling out $60 an hour, sometimes three times a week, for sessions with a private acting coach, something I was scared into doing every time I had an audition. The private coach was an attractive, forceful woman in her early forties who kept in great shape and was a bit rough around the edges. I'll call her "Claudette." Claudette was a cross between Mrs. Robinson and Kathleen Turner. She had a strange hold on me. She would warn me in pretty harsh terms of the irreparable harm I could do to my career if I messed up even one audition, but reassured me that she had gotten to me in time and could help me take advantage of the avenues I hadn't yet damaged.

Acting class may have taught me some things, but I'm glad eventually I got out and didn't become another one of its permanent students. For me at least, I started getting booked for acting jobs when I stopped with the classes. Nowhere else in real life did I beat myself up as much, analyze everything to death, and feel so inadequate as I was encouraged to do in acting class. Even though I already beat myself up and analyzed myself to death, acting lessons brought this art to a whole new self-destructive level. But it took me a long time to figure that out. Of course the parts I auditioned for never had anything to do with all that deep stuff I did in class: all the crying, the pretending you're slipping on ice, the screaming and shoving matches, or remembering the pain the time Uncle Larry threw a book of stamps at you. And in the end I would get parts the way most comedians do, by reenacting my stand-up persona. But it would take a lot of auditioning to get there.

6

AUDITIONS

My first audition was for a TV pilot in 1988 that never aired. All I remember was that it was about two buddies and I had to do a sinister laugh. I got to the lot early, found a pay phone, and called my friend Joel in Brooklyn. I practiced my laugh for Joel a few times so he could reassure me that it was, in fact, maniacal and authentic. If that wasn't enough confirmation, I only had to look at the man standing behind me who had been waiting to use the phone. The look on his face assured me I seemed like quite the lunatic.

In the waiting room, I recognized Michael Cole, the star of the sixties hit classic *The Mod Squad*. He sensed that I was freaking out, and although I knew he hadn't worked much since *Mod Squad*, he was kind enough to offer help by running my lines with me before I went in. That was the first of a very few times I'd get unsolicited help from a competing actor.

My first two years out West, I stumbled through most of my auditions without a clue as to why I could never book anything. Here's how it goes: The first step is usually the call from the agent informing me of the appointment, and then I'd get faxed the sides, the extracted section of the script with the lines I'd be doing at the audition. Back in 1988 when I came out for my first pilot season, I didn't have a fax machine, so I had to drive a half hour to the William Morris Agency in Beverly Hills to pick up my sides.

My agent was not very inspiring. Once I found myself being put up for the part of a southern redneck.

"Are you sure this is the right part I'm supposed to read for?" I asked my agent. "It doesn't seem to make sense."

"It's in their best interest to use you," he said, looking at me for just a brief second before turning his head toward the beautiful garden right outside his window. "Just have fun with it. Have fun with your audition."

Fun? I had no idea how to make the arduous process fun. To me, auditions are as uncomfortable as having to apply for college several times a month for years on end. It's like being on a date, where they're just sort of laughing at the things you say and there's a long line of others right behind you waiting to charm them. As far as the odds for success, it's like being a traveling salesman who only sells one tchotchke every few months if he's lucky.

To make matters worse, finding my way around L.A. was not easy, especially after I first arrived. I was used to New York, where the streets are numbered and straight. I had found that the stress of being late or lost would totally defuse any preparation I had put into the audition. Many times I would drive to the casting office the night before as a rehearsal to assure myself I knew the correct path.

But often, getting to the actual studio wasn't the end of the headache. I'd be on a big studio lot such as Paramount or Twentieth Century Fox and the parking structure seemed to be a mile away from where the audition was. The security guard would give me a map and use his yellow highlighter to outline the path to my destination. Except I'm map illiterate; they're so complicated. And a studio lot has all sorts of little streets that aren't really streets: "Make a left on Clark Gable Way and turn right by the monument to Mickey Rooney, and then you go through two double doors."

There's always those double doors. And they all look alike. Inevitably, I'd get confused and find myself on actual sets only to have some assistant director wearing headphones curse me out. Once in a while, I'd get lucky and bump into another actor trying to find the same place and we would go on the maddening journey together. Once, another actor told me he was late and ran ahead when I asked him for directions. But he had that beady look in his eyes. I didn't trust him. I don't think he was late; he just didn't want to help me. His odds of getting the job would improve if one less actor found the place.

Eventually, somehow I'd find the audition. It always turns out that whenever I kill myself to get to an audition, like I'm rushing to defuse a bomb, they're a half an hour behind schedule anyway.

Afterwards I'd see other frantic actors walking around with their highlighted maps looking for their appointment. It looked like the lot was littered with actors using their little treasure maps to find their way to a pot of gold. Most of the gold on these treasure hunts didn't come in a pot anyway. A week on a show after taxes and commission was about $3,600. When that happens a few times a year, if you're lucky, it ends up amounting to about a thimble of gold. Not terrible, but not the biggest jackpot. A pilot, now that's a big jackpot. That could be about twenty grand, even if it doesn't go to series. Usually, they pay all that money to keep you off the market for other pilots.

I used to try to prepare not only my sides, but also my casual banter before and after my reading. This never worked. My acting teacher once told us when Danny DeVito auditioned for the show *Taxi*, he came in and threw down the script and said, "Who wrote this crap?" He was not just auditioning for the part of the crude Louie De Palma, he *was* him! So in '88, when I auditioned for the part of a nervous office boy on Richard Lewis' show *Anything but Love*, I thought I had something great to play with. The casting woman had a small dog right there in her office. I came in trembling like I was too afraid to enter with her pet there. "Is it okay, will he attack me? Will he lunge at me?" I asked as I carefully slunk into her office, walking as if I were on the ledge of a skyscraper. I could see the look on the casting woman's face. She was perplexed, but I felt I had to stick with my failing gimmick. I was too embarrassed to bail out in the middle and say, "I'm not really scared of the dog. I thought this would show how in character I am. But maybe I was wrong. Maybe the character isn't afraid of everything. Yup, I overdid it." After that failure, I never again did anything before a reading that would make people wonder about my mental health.

It's also easy to get thrown off because not only do you see all the competition in the waiting area, sometimes, if the walls are thin, you even have to hear them. This happened the time I was supposed to read for a little part where all I had to do was ask someone if I could get a ride with them. They tell me they aren't going my way, and then I plead, "Come on. I love convertibles!" I was feeling fairly comfortable because I told myself that there wasn't much I could do with those lines anyway. I'd just give it my best shot. They called in the guy before me and I was faintly able to hear him saying the words I was about to say next. But what I did hear clearly was laughter erupting from the room that sounded like the loudest laugh track I had ever heard on a sitcom, followed by a fervent round of applause. When it was my turn, I couldn't concentrate. All I could think of was "How the hell could that guy have gotten those uproarious laughs with this same stuff?"

At least these people were polite. They mostly always are. It's the bad, brutal auditions that stick with you. Once, a casting agent was leading me into a room to read for some producers of a new show. She gave very specific instructions about who would and would not shake my hand.

"Now don't be offended that Karen, the producer, and Mark, the assistant producer, will not shake your hand, but Willie, the director, will, and so will Randy, the other producer."

Now I'm freaking out trying to retain that information. I'm already in the room and I forget who I can shake with and who I can't. "Okay," I tell myself, "just make it easier and don't shake anyone's hand." But then, I wonder if the people with whom I could shake would be offended if I don't extend my hand to them. What other interview or meeting has these rules? Where else are you informed that certain people you'll be meeting do not wish to humanize you and just want to view you as some talking matter momentarily passing through?

Sometimes an audition is just for the casting person, otherwise known as a pre-read. If the casting agent thinks you're worthy of the next step, then you read for the producers. I have been on many auditions where the pre-read is the same day as the producers' session. An actor will read and on their way out the casting agent asks the assistant to give him information about where the producers' session is. I know I'm dead right away when I have auditioned and don't get any producer session information.

When the pot of gold is the possibility of a pilot for a new series, the third and final step is auditioning for the network brass, otherwise known as "going to network." But that's not just one audition. I went to network for a Chris Elliott pilot after which they told me to wait outside for a while. They then had each of us auditioning for the same part come back in and read with various wives they were considering. Then we had to wait outside again and one at a time come back in and stand next to various actors, who'd play our kids, to see if we looked like we were related. All of this square-dancing didn't matter because I wasn't cast and the pilot didn't get picked up anyway.

I didn't even make it as far as the producers' session when I auditioned for the nerd on the NBC show *Dear John* my first year in LA. Claudette, my acting coach, really laid into me for what a juicy opportunity I'd missed.

"You only went as far as casting?! Too bad I wasn't coaching you then. That show became a hit. I could have at least gotten you to network, maybe even gotten you on the show!"

True to form, she then reassured me I can forget about *Dear John* and that the best was all ahead. She gave me knowledge and assurance and tips and everything but the confidence that I could ever tackle any kind of audition on my own. She wanted me to feel dependent. After an audition, she'd call me, and I'd have to give her beat for beat feedback about how I did each and every line. She'd reinforce how it seemed I did great and how she was the reason behind it.

And I bought it. I was convinced that if I ever so much as tried to audition without her coaching, it would be my last one. She hammered into me that without her help, if I had a bad audition, word would get around that I was a waste of a casting director's time. I'd be blackballed and there are thousands of other actors just dying to get that shot at *Charles in Charge*.

I accepted all of this because I was like so many desperate, scared people who came to Los Angeles hoping for their shot. And she knew how to keep me more scared and more dependent. She'd always drop the names of big stars, like cast members of *Twin Peaks* who had gotten their break because of her work. She'd repeatedly point out that I wasn't getting any younger and how time was of the essence. She'd give me tips on what to wear. She'd hint of the massive contacts with big producers she had and when I was ready, she'd set some up.

I knew something was off about our relationship, that ours was not a healthy dynamic, but I still was not confident enough to let her go, especially when something very big happened: I finally got my first acting part.

7

WORST FIRST

I didn't start out expecting to be a perennial guest star. In fact, my first time ever on the set of a TV show, I was going to be a series regular. The way it came about, I thought this TV business was going to be pretty easy. Instead, I nearly didn't survive my first week.

I walked into my first network audition in April 1989. Luckily I had no idea I was going to be in front of the most famous TV executive in America, so I didn't have time to get anxious about it. All I knew was I had passed the preliminary cut for a Mel Brooks pilot about a wacky hotel called *The Nutt House*. Now I had to be approved by network honchos. When I got to NBC studios in Burbank and looked around the room at the fifteen people deciding my fate, I recognized one right away—Brandon Tartikoff, who was so young and hip he'd appeared as himself on *Saturday Night Live* and *Night Court* and been profiled in *Rolling Stone*.

Mel Brooks was not there. I wish I could remember the lines; it was just me timidly answering a few questions from my stern supervisor. Mostly they were one-word responses. Maybe I can say what clicked is what usually makes something work in an audition. Something just connects when you walk through the door before you even read the lines. Something out of your or any coach's control.

I didn't get the part of the dopey bellhop at The Nutt House Hotel, but my agent said I came close and made an impression. Shortly thereafter, the casting woman from NBC showed Tartikoff my video demo reel (the one Billy Crystal didn't want to see). It had clips of me doing my act on some cable shows and bits I did when I was on David Brenner's show. Tartikoff must've liked me because he suggested me to the producers of a new NBC show, *Singer & Sons*, about a New York deli, that had received an order for four episodes. My audition was set up for the creator of the show who had previous success at the helm of the hits *Charles in Charge* and *My Two Dads*. I had just a few lines, portraying Sheldon Singer, who worked in the deli owned by his uncle.

There wasn't much to the role. I had to be nervously explaining to my uncle that I had prepared a sandwich the correct way. I thought I'd lost the part because I wasn't called back to audition again. Then a few weeks later when I got the call that I had booked the show, it was an utter shock. Apparently NBC was so behind me that they had pushed me through without another audition. I would be making $7,000 an episode! That was the most I had ever earned for one week of work, but my joy lasted only until I called Claudette, trying to share my good news.

"I knew all my hard work would pay off," Claudette said. "See what coaching did for you? Do you see?"

I then heard her flipping through the pages of what had to be her appointment book.

"Okay, I'm pretty booked up, but I think I can squeeze you in. We should do at least three sessions this week."

I was baffled. "I got the job. What do I have to come in this week for?"

And then I heard what sounded like the loudest, most disappointed sigh.

"I know many actors who got what they thought was their break only to be replaced after one day of rehearsal because they were a beat or two off," she said ominously. "Lots of money is spent on these shows, and if you give them any reason to think they made a mistake, out you will go! You stop with the coaching now, you're going to lose everything we've worked on, and you'll go right back to what you were before we started. And you were not doing so good before you met me, were you?"

I was too inexperienced not to fall for her head trip, but I can't give her full credit for all my fear. The executive producer of the show was doing an equally stellar job of making me feel inadequate.

Most sitcoms are a five-day workweek, but this one had a few extra days because it was a pilot and needed more time to get into shape. The first day starts with a table read (a reading of the first draft of the script), where the cast sits around a long table with the director and producers at the end. There are name placards indicating which actors are supposed to sit where, and chairs surrounding the table for network and production company executives, and anyone else involved with the show.

On most shows, before the reading begins, the director or showrunner makes a rousing speech. I would later learn that if it's a show already in production, usually they can talk about how great their last episode was or their ratings or awards or reviews. But this was a brand new show, so the showrunner's speech was especially impassioned. He stated that it was the start of something very special that would impact so many people's lives. He talked about how thrilled he was that such a strong, unique ensemble cast of characters had been put together. Then each cast member was introduced to a hearty round of applause.

Harold Gould, a veteran actor who I knew from the sitcom *Rhoda* and the Woody Allen film *Love and Death*, starred as Mr. Singer, the owner of the deli, who had no sons to take it over. Esther Rolle, an African American actress who had previously played a maid on *Maude*, a character she then spun-off into her own series, *Good Times*, was once again playing a maid. This time, she was Harold Gould's longtime, loyal maid. Her two sons would be the ones to inherit the deli. The joke was to be these black guys running a Jewish deli—a concept that was either radical and forward-thinking about race and prejudice or ridiculously contrived, depending on your viewpoint and the writing. Mitchell was the responsible single dad and Reggie was the free-spirited radical. There was also a sassy, pretty black waitress who spoke Yiddish. I was Harold Gould's nephew, who was way too moronic to inherit the deli.

At the table reading, the laughs were huge. It felt as if we were at a pep rally to give the world the next comedy dynasty—a *Cheers* or *Taxi*. Unfortunately, this feeling did not last once we got on the set and started the week of rehearsals.

Before this, I had never even visited a set, so it was all new and exciting for me. The main set was the deli itself. In typical three-camera sitcom style, there were rooms with one side sliced off for the studio audience and cameras to see. The focal point of the set was the deli counter. Off to the side was Mr. Singer's apartment.

Esther Rolle didn't seem thrilled to be part of the show. On the set she was very cordial, but spent most of her breaks in her room. She confided to me she had played too many maids and wasn't eager to play another one. But like anyone, she preferred to be working than not. She opened up with how frustrating her last few seasons on *Good Times* were. She resented the silly direction the show had gone in from its roots as a social commentary on a lower-class black family. She reenacted for me a scene in which her son, played by Jimmie J. J. Walker, was supposed to simply take an apple out of the refrigerator but hammed it up with a lot of over the top mugging while he pondered what food was there. I was trying not to laugh, because what she found offensive and clownish was funny to me. I was already partial to Walker because of when I first saw him on TV. I had never seen anyone like him. He wasn't like the pretty teens on all the other shows I watched growing up like *The Partridge Family* and *The Brady Bunch*. He was skinny and goofy-looking like I was.

I remember the guest actors were all hopeful that they would reappear on the show too, if it were to be picked up. I sat with them at lunch and overheard all of their nervous desperation:

"I was a cop, so if there's ever a problem again in the deli, they'll bring me back I hope."

"I'm the third lead's uncle. I think I'm in because I'm related to a cast regular!"

"I ordered the fruit salad. Maybe that's what I could be known as: The Guy Who Eats the Fruit Salad."

Little did I know that for the next twenty years, all of my hopes would be just like those of these needy guest actors. Like the guy who ordered the fruit salad, I'd always hope that any small connection to the show would be enough to get me back on.

Each day, we'd rehearse the scenes with just the director. At the end of the day, the producers would come to the set for a run-through that for me quickly became a dreaded event. When the assistant director would shout out, "Ten minutes to run-through!" as he set up the row of director chairs in front of the deli set where the top brass would sit and watch, I'd tremble with fear. No live performance of any kind felt as pressurized as that little row of bodies with their notepads in hand, scrutinizing every nuance of the show. When this gang of producers finally did come to the set, it felt as if the bullies had invaded the playground, ready to negate any fun we might have been having. Suddenly I felt like a non-person. When I tried to say hi to the showrunner, he snubbed me; he seemed more worried about the props. Entire sections were totally rewritten. The filming was delayed because some felt it wasn't ready. There was even talk that the whole thing might be scrapped. The more run-throughs we had, the more time everyone had to get nervous and pick the show apart. The showrunner was a nervous guy to begin with, and the network couldn't afford to be casual when they've invested millions of dollars in a new series.

After each run-through, we'd get syllable-by-syllable notes on how to do each line. The showrunner told the black guys how to talk "blacker." I felt uncomfortable watching this preppy little guy with glasses strut and bob his head precisely demonstrating the proper lingo and movements: "Yo, Shell! You-be-cool-bro!" I wondered if the black guys were offended, but they just said, "Got it" and took the notes.

I just had a few lines. My big moment occurred when a black guy came in for the first time, and I had to act terrified, as if he was going to rob the place. But I would get conflicting notes from one run-through to the next. I'd do what the director had told me to do during rehearsals, and then in the notes session get chewed out by the showrunner for being so off. Once he said that the viewers would change the channel because of me. The director never came to my defense. When I told him that I was confused, he just told me that I had better get it together and stop being so nervous.

After run-throughs, the writers retreated to their offices for long hours of rewriting. The production assistants would deliver the revised scripts in manila envelopes to the actors' homes either late that night or early the next morning. I kept waking up in the middle of the night and reaching outside my door for that envelope to see what lines of mine had survived from that day's run-through. I remember leafing through the script and freaking out when I'd see lines that I thought I hit the day before had been cut. Now I know that scripts always start a little long so lines will be trimmed as the week progresses and the first ones to lose lines are the secondary characters, but to this day, even if I know I had a great run-through, I'll always worry about getting cut. And back then, I was really a nervous wreck.

With good reason, it turned out. The most horrifying run-through of *Singer & Sons* came just a few days before we were finally going to tape. Afterwards, I did not get one note, and that just did not seem right. I went over to the showrunner and asked if what I did was okay. He made no eye contact and walked right past me as if I were dead. I freaked out. I needed reassuring, so

I sought out the woman who was tutoring the young actress on the show and had worked with the showrunner before. She was blunt. She said that it looked like I was gone. She said that's the way it's been with him on his other shows. No notes, you're off.

I rushed home and called my agent. He confirmed the bad news. The showrunner wanted to fire me. But why? The agent could only speculate. "Why do you think?" he asked.

"Maybe I was nervous. I admit that. But everyone is telling me something different, or they're completely ignoring me."

My agent had some sobering ideas. "You know what, I don't think this guy wanted you, even from the beginning. He created the show and had a vision of your character, and then the network thrust you upon him."

"Then why'd he hire me in the first place?"

"This happens more than you know. Sometimes a producer will not fight the network at the start to get their project green-lit, and then they might have their first choice waiting in the wings once it's off and running. He might have been auditioning others for your role even after you were cast. But sit tight. The network's trying to convince him to let you stay on."

That whole weekend I was a mess of insecurity and self-loathing, but in the end they did convince him to let me stay. I was still nervous knowing I wasn't to his liking, but was relieved as all hell to still be there. Esther Rolle took me aside and gave me little pep talks. "Don't let anyone in show business ever determine your self-worth. You're wonderful."

On tape night the audience was packed, mostly with those who were bused in from various Hollywood tourist spots and been handed tickets by guys with the job I once had.

What they try to downplay when pawning off the tickets is that a half-hour show usually takes three to five hours to tape. Not only did a new or little-known show have to bus its crowds in, they often had to feed them and sometimes even had to pay them to sit through the taping. Later in my career I witnessed studio ushers having to escort out deranged, screaming homeless people from the audience. They probably got in because the ticket guys were desperate to earn their money by getting any warm bodies into the seats.

Why does everything take so long? Each scene that you see is done at least two times to get different camera coverage. And after a scene, the writers will converge on the set and try to come up with funnier lines right there on the spot. Sometimes these huddles could take as long as half an hour. There's a warm-up host, usually a stand-up comic, who has to keep the crowd hanging in there by tossing out candy bars, T-shirts, and praying someone has a birthday so the audience can all sing "Happy Birthday." One time, I could swear he stretched by having everyone sing "Happy Birthday" to someone who had one coming up in two weeks.

During the taping, the few lines I had seemed to click. The showrunner, my one-time adversary, began warming up to me. He shook my hand for the first time, finally not afraid that acknowledging me in any way would indicate he wanted me around. With a big smile, he told me I had done a great job. But I made a mistake and told my acting coach about my close call. I should have expected Claudette's response.

"Now do you see how crucial it is you get coached?"

Claudette did have a nurturing side. She was not this dour Nurse Ratched—more like a seductress from a horror film. On tape night of that first episode, she had been there on set cheering me on. She watched me do my first scene and hugged me afterwards.

"I am so proud of you. You have come so far. Now we have just three more shows to get through, sweetie. Call me when you have the next script. We got to get working on it as soon as possible."

It wasn't easy for me to sever the ties. I was still traumatized from my near-firing. I got coached for the next three episodes, but was getting more resentful. And Claudette doubled her fee. She informed me that coaching for a part is an entirely different, more involved process than coaching for an audition. But, of course, it was because she knew I had money now. I told myself to just pay the new fee and know I had done everything I could. The producers may have gained some confidence in me, but my parts were still very small. In one of the episodes, I had two lines and had to high five one of the "cool" black guys. That hour Claudette worked me over and over on it. I was paying double the normal fee to have this theater professional carefully evaluate my high five.

"Do it again. Fred, do it again but extend the arm higher and straighter."

So I did it, and she said, "Much better. That's the way to high five!" That's how insecure this business makes you feel—that you need to pay for high five lessons.

The run-throughs got a little less scary for me over the next three episodes. The mood on the set relaxed just a little. The series regulars talked about possible time slots that might be good for the show and hopes of real estate purchases should it become a success.

After the four episodes were done, the showrunner seemed glad I was kept on after all. Apparently, I had delivered an awesome high five. I am a big enough man to give credit to the coach, if that is what did it. Unfortunately, my high five wasn't awesome enough to save the show. It aired on Saturday night for four weeks in June of 1990. I remember checking the paper when the weekly Nielsen ratings were posted and having to look far down the list to find our show. It probably only got the attention of die hard *Empty Nest* fans, who were livid that for four weeks, their beloved show was preempted for something called *Singer & Sons*. It died a quick death and most likely did little to help heal race relations as some on the set had envisioned.

Since my casting had been so swift, I thought it would only be matter of time before I got another full-time gig. Instead, more than twenty years later, *Singer & Sons* remains the only time that I've had the chance to be a regular on a new series. It also remains the most tense set I've ever been on. And I'm glad, because after that, almost every show has been great by comparison. Worried about finances, I decided right then that I was done with acting coaches. There was no ugly confrontation when I broke it off. I just stopped calling, and thankfully, she didn't track me down to ask why. I told myself that it just wasn't worth it. I had decided that auditions were all so arbitrary anyway that it made as much sense as paying someone to coach you on how to pull the lever on a slot machine.

8

OTHER PEOPLE'S HOMES

Neglecting to tell me I had been booked for a week of work just days away was the last straw in my deteriorating relationship with the William Morris Agency. The agent who had originally taken me on had moved to another department, and I had been "dropped in the lap" of another agent. I'd soon find out being dropped onto someone's lap isn't always a good thing. People like when something or someone is their own discovery. This agent had an oversized roster of clients he had passionately found and carefully placed on his own lap. The William Morris Agency is huge. If you aren't a hot commodity with a production deal or a name like Brad Pitt or Tom Hanks, it's not just easy to get lost in the shuffle, it's almost guaranteed.

If the wardrobe lady hadn't called for my sizes a few days in advance, I would've been in a depressing comedy condo in Dayton, Ohio, trying to decide which of three mustard containers in the fridge contained the least bacteria as my name was being introduced at the table read of *Lenny*. This would be my first network guest appearance since *Singer & Sons*. In that seven months since I played Sheldon, the timid deli guy, half that money I earned had gone to taxes, living expenses, and the rest to my agent and coach.

The role I was to play was in a new show featuring Lenny Clarke, a stand-up comedian who had immense popularity in his hometown of Boston. In his self-titled show *Lenny* he played a good-natured working-class lug, working two jobs trying to make good for his family. Mainly he worked for the electric company, but at night sometimes moonlighted as a doorman at a fancy hotel. I'd be playing the bellhop.

The set was a great contrast to the stress and panic from the *Singer & Sons* set. At the run-throughs, the producers were very accessible, greeting me and telling me I was doing a good job. After the first run-through, Lenny mentioned there was a good chance they'd "bring me back." That was the first time someone said that to me. I remembered that on *Singer & Sons*, that was the magic phrase the fruit salad guy longed to hear.

Only the show was not doing well in the ratings, but everyone on the set was still fairly optimistic. Just a few more episodes were produced after my appearance and I never did return.

"What the hell's *Lenny*?" was the first thing my mother asked when I told her I was on it, and that was what most people who saw it on my résumé also wanted to know. But it was significant to me because I got that part on my own without any coaching. And it also lit the fire in me to leave my agent and find one who, like me, felt getting booked on a show as a cackling dopey bellhop was something worth noting.

9

AMEN TO GREAT FOOD!

Most of the hard work in an acting career is actually landing the job. No stress compares to the uncertainty of wanting to fill all of those vacant boxes on one's month-at-a-glance calendar. So when I got offered a role on the sitcom *Amen* without having to audition, it was a real compliment, an actor's dream. But it also made me even more nervous. At least if I'd auditioned, I'd know that they liked what I did. Instead I was flying blind.

It turned out the executive producer was familiar with my Thrill Seeker persona from some of the stand-up cable shows I had done. They had gotten a video of my jokes and decided that I didn't have to read for the part. They even asked for permission to use several of my jokes in the dialogue.

The star of *Amen* was Sherman Hemsley, famous for playing George Jefferson on *The Jeffersons*, now playing Deacon Ernest Frye, who didn't quite see eye to eye with his church's new young minister, played by Clifton Davis. My episode was titled "The Wild Deak," a parody of the Brando movie *The Wild One*. I played one of two biker thug brothers who harass the ministers at a food stop. I was the puny one who pretends to be tough but really lets his brother, a menacing psycho, do the dirty work. It was the most lines I had ever been given in the highest-profile show I had ever done. And so, nearly a year after my liberation from my coach, I had a relapse. Although I still resented her for how manipulative she was, I thought I needed professional reassurance before I read at the table.

I stood outside her fairly modest home in the San Fernando Valley, which was built on the fears and desperation of many actors like me. She walked a young actor out the door and gave him some extra free words of encouragement as I approached the steps, "Good-bye sweetie. You'll be great. Call me and let me know how it goes."

I felt a little something like the battered spouse who comes back to the abusive ex. I rationalized that I had done dozens of auditions and gotten *Lenny* on my own, so what's the big deal if I needed this little boost?

She took me back in and didn't openly chide me for leaving her, though I did notice a slight smirk on her face. But her coaching on my *Amen* scene assured me that I'd never break my vow again. She was way, way off. They'd cast me because I was a wimp, and she misread the part as if I were supposed to be a thug. Claudette had instructed me to act with menacing, powerful authority. "Show them who you are!"

The table read seemed to go okay, and the writers seemed to be in a good mood as they headed off to their offices to make minor adjustments based on the reading. It didn't appear they'd have to spend many hours tweaking the script into better shape. *Amen* was a show that just had to stay above the radar and last long enough to produce the hundred or so episodes needed to reach syndication. But as I made my way to the food table, Don Gibb, the actor portraying Cashmere, my crazy biker brother, pulled me aside. Gibb, a big, bushy-haired guy with a lazy eye who looked like a WWF villain, is best known for his role as the bully in the

Revenge of the Nerds movies. He looked at me intently with that one eye of his.

"What did you do, man? What were you doing there?"

"What are you talking about?"

"I've seen your act. You should just be yourself. You're so funny. You were being too big for the part. Drop it down a notch, man. Do what you do at the clubs."

I couldn't believe it. This guy, whose signature piece was pounding his chest as he snarled and convulsed while screaming, "Nerds! I hate Nerds!" was telling me I was playing something too big. But he was right, and I felt like a fool telling him why I took it in that over-the-top direction. I suppose if Claudette had told me that it was as simple as Don Gibb told me it was, she wouldn't be getting my checks.

"Be yourself. The acting comes out in the lines. Just say them. It's not science. You're funny. You shouldn't have to push it ever."

I almost wanted to take out my wallet and give him all the cash I had on me for finally curing me of Claudette.

At rehearsals, the producers echoed his thoughts in a very calm, reassuring way. They were not panicked at all. They also told me to be myself, to be deadpan like my act. It felt great throwing out my sides that were covered with all of her over-the-top instructions.

As the week progressed, I started to enjoy myself, after all, I was playing a version of my stand-up persona.

"You better listen to me," I told Helmsley, "because I drank milk that expired yesterday! And I went to a deli and ate an apple right there without washing it first!" After that scene, Sherman Hemsley would point his finger at me, laugh heartily, and say, "You're funny. You are a funny man!"

At the time, I wasn't aware of how rare it was to be actually saying some of my own words on a sitcom. Usually, the material you're handed each day is pretty set in stone. The actors, especially the guest actors, aren't encouraged to stray from what's on the page. Script supervisors read the text at the taping and rehearsals to make sure every word is being said exactly the way it's supposed to be said in the script. They'll run up to you after a take is over and show you their script if you are a little bit off. Some shows are so strict, the script supervisor will point out if you missed an "um" or if you said "okay" instead of "all right."

Lunchtime came after our first day of rehearsal and I headed toward the door. Roz Ryan, who played the loquacious member of the church board, was on line with several of her other fellow cast members. "Where you going, motorcycle man?" she asked.

"To the commissary for lunch."

"Why don't you want to eat here with us? Are you too good for us?"

"I'm allowed to eat lunch with you here?"

"Of course! What are you talking about?"

"Well, I just did this show called *Lenny* and during the week, only regular cast members got free lunches. Guests had to go out."

That was true. During the week, production assistants came by and took the lunch orders for just the regulars, who would leisurely select a choice meal, while I stood by trying to not glance at the tasty treasures on the menu that were forbidden to me.

She put her arm around me and guided me to the lunch line. "Honey, this ain't no *Lenny*! This ain't no *Lenny* here."

Her invitation started a tradition with my friend Joel in Brooklyn that would not go away. Joel has been my best friend since we were seventeen. We bonded instantly in the neighborhood when we realized we both were overwhelmed underachievers from dysfunctional families who still wanted something better than what we saw around us. I call Joel "The Fugitive" because, like the TV character, he's a bright guy who goes from terrible job to terrible job where his coworkers can never understand why he's working there. He's been bald since age twenty-three, wears big round glasses, and surprisingly is only twenty pounds overweight for someone that probably spends 86 percent of his waking life thinking about and craving food.

Some shows serve the guests free lunches during the week and some don't. But all shows serve a free meal on tape night at least. So from there on in, whatever show I was on, Joel had to know what free food I got. It was like I was eating vicariously for him. He cared about that much more than my tales of showbiz.

After a while, Joel's wife grew a little resentful of me. During dinner, he'd be on the phone moaning in ecstasy, hearing my description of his favorite baby back ribs, while she was serving him frozen fish sticks. Years later, if I ever mentioned a show I'd been on, he'd joyfully reminisce about the scrumptious meal they had offered, as if it were he who had eaten it.

"Joel, can you believe the enormous contracts the guys from *Friends* got?"

"*Friends*: Salmon baked well with hard crunchy edges and Oreo ice-cream cookies melted with hot fudge for dessert!"

I ran into trouble on *Amen* on the night of taping, not because of my acting but because of my physique. The makeup guy had a tantrum because my arm was too thin for him to put on a fake tattoo. Frustrated, he tried different ones, but most were too large, so he cursed and kicked a chair. He then claimed he wasn't mad at me, just at the assholes that cast me.

But the taping went well. From what I've seen, when a stand-up comedian does his material in the context of a show, it always looks rather fake, like a show within a show. I felt that way about my part, but the crowd ate it up. When I ordered my big brother, Cashmere, to cause major bodily harm to the heroes of *Amen*, the Deacon stood up to Cashmere and punched him in the stomach as the crowd went wild. Then Jester Hairston, who played Rolly, the wise ninety-year-old church board member, raised his fist to me, and I ran out screaming for dear life.

The cast and producers thanked me for my week on the show and a producer suggested to Don Gibb and me that it would be "a kick to get the two of you back." I knew that would be a stretch but I didn't even have time to imagine ways that my biker brother and I could return, because shortly after our appearance, *Amen,* having made its requisite number of episodes for syndication, meandered into the TV graveyard. I was back on the audition circuit.

10

MURPHY BROWN

In 1991, I hadn't actually seen an episode of *Murphy Brown,* but I knew it was a critically acclaimed top-rated show. And from the overheard discussions of the competing actors in the crowded casting session I was on, I learned it was one of a few shows that was not very inclusive to the guest casts passing through.

"My friend did *Murphy Brown* a few weeks ago. He said the regulars are really cold to the guests."

"Yeah, I heard that too," another actor offered.

"But the coldest set I ever worked on had to be *Night Court.* Harry Anderson is not a good guy."

"Harry Anderson?" I asked. "I did a few stand-up gigs with him a long time ago. He seemed like a great guy."

"When was that? Have you worked with him lately? I tried talking to him, it was like, 'What do you want from me?' And John Larroquette, our scenes were together all week and not once on a break would he say hello or even give me eye contact."

"Have any of you worked on *Cheers*?" Another actor chimed in. "There were two different camps of regulars that hung out with each other. And none of them hardly acknowledged the guests."

As much as I was enjoying the guest star war stories of the journeymen alongside me, I excused myself to step outside to concentrate on the material. Like *Singer & Sons*, the airing of *Amen* and its inclusion on my demo reel failed to send my career into the stratosphere. I spent nine months afterwards in a state of unease and unemployment, desperately trying to affirm some positive or negative big star interactions of my own. This was a part I wanted—actually I wanted any part. I was auditioning for the part of one of Murphy's many secretaries. This one was supposed to be an obnoxious, hack comedian walking around the office doing dozens of lame jokes.

I was still new enough that I had to first audition for Andrea Cohen, the casting director, before being seen by any of the producers. After watching me she stared, confused. "That's an interesting way to go. It's supposed to be a typical, annoying comedian, but you read it as if you were a special-ed kid, who's pathetic and takes night courses on how to be a comedian."

Obviously, she didn't realize that I was basically just being me, but that's not a bad way to describe how I probably come off in most things I do.

She kept staring at my résumé, quizzically, like a doctor looking over a patient's chart. Finally, she said: "Know what I'm going to do, if you don't mind? Can you do what you just did again? I'm going to bring someone in from next door to take a look at it." Huh, I thought. I must have been so different from what the producers had envisioned that she needed a second opinion. Little did I know she'd be calling in a specialist.

The woman who came in from next door turned out to be Deedee Bradley, the casting director for the drama *Life Goes On*—a show about the life of Corky, a tenacious kid with Down syndrome. Suddenly, I wasn't as concerned about getting the job as I was about convincing these two women that I wasn't mocking the mentally challenged, or wasn't mentally challenged myself. The last thing I wanted was for Deedee to say, "That's not funny, that's what we do on *our* show."

For a moment, I thought about doing it differently, but risked coming off even more insensitive. So I read it again the same way. When I finished, I looked up from my script, awaiting the diagnosis. Deedee smiled, turned to Andrea, and said, "It's funny." I'm sure all three of us were relieved.

The next day, I came back and auditioned for the producers. The show's Diane English was one of the few showrunners who had become a household name. To me, the room looked like her and a clump of other people out of focus. You could tell she was in charge. I felt the same kind of pressure I felt auditioning for Brandon Tartikoff at NBC. I could try to pretend that she wasn't there, but it would be impossible.

I read the lines the way I did the day before, maniacally and pathetically. They seemed intrigued. They had me step out, come back in, and do it again.

I didn't get the part. I was a little disappointed, but my agent conveyed to me that the producers loved me and it would be just a matter of time before they found a spot for me on *Murphy Brown*. I was naïve enough to be excited about what I believed was the undeniable impression I had made. I was informed the part ended up going to a comic who more fit the prototype of the annoying, "always on" comic. I instinctively knew most shows don't stray from the breakdown description of the guest star parts. Now I try not to take it so personally when I am passed over for an audition when I know I'm way off from what they're looking for.

A few weeks later, I'd get another chance with *Murphy Brown*. I auditioned for another part. It was for an usher who wouldn't let Frank Fontana, one of the reporters of "FYI," the show-within-the-show, played by Joe Regalbuto, into an awards show. Frank was up for an award, but had forgotten his ticket. My whole job was to rebuff him with the mantra, "I need a ticket."

"You don't understand," he'd plead. "I want to just peek in and then I'll come back."

"I need a ticket."

"Don't you know who I am? I'm up for an award."

(Long beat) "I don't think so. Ticket please!"

This part I did get. I felt connected when I came in for the producers who had enjoyed my version of the "always on" comedian a few weeks ago. Most times I have found that what nails a part is a prior favorable audition or performance, and that the reading is almost secondary. The role is preconceived in your favor.

My new agents were thrilled because *Murphy Brown* was at that time a top sitcom and a great way to end my long dry spell they had stuck with me through. I had actually been recommended to them by the New York William Morris agent who had initially signed me. He told me that William Morris was too big and that I'd be better off at a smaller agency, known in the industry as a "boutique agency."

After expecting to be shunned from any off-stage contact with the reported icy cold regulars of *Murphy Brown*, I was pleasantly surprised to find they were very open to me. Only the show's star, Candice Bergen, didn't really fraternize during breaks at rehearsals. She'd usually rush off to her trailer, followed by her assistant, who would hand her the set's cordless phone (this was the pre-cellular era), as a way for her to ward off all around her.

Part of me still felt like a fan who had been let in off the street, a feeling I think I conveyed a little too much when I met Joe Regalbuto before rehearsing our scene together. I excitedly complimented him on his cameo film work of the early eighties, including playing the pedophile murderer in *The Star Chamber*. I couldn't tell if he found my familiarity with his résumé flattering or frightening.

One of the perks of being on these shows is getting to invite friends, agents, or prospective girlfriends to tapings. A production assistant informed me that I was only allotted two tickets for the Friday night taping. *Murphy Brown* was a hot ticket. They didn't have to bus in half-medicated audience members and shove Hershey bars in their mouths to keep them awake for the long tapings.

I decided to pass on the tickets. After three years in Los Angeles, I didn't have many friends in town who would sit in the bleachers to support me. Most of my contacts were embittered, jaded comics. I could understand how frustrating it would be to watch four hours of something you're not in, if not much else is going on in your career. And at the time there weren't any promising potential dates, especially not someone who I would feel comfortable having sit through a lengthy taping for my few minutes onstage.

I opened up about this to Grant Shaud, who played Miles Silverberg, the high-strung neurotic producer of "FYI."

"People think it should be easy for me to get a nice woman because I've been on TV a few times, but it's not."

"Tell me about it," he said, shaking his head.

I was happy for the empathy, but also taken aback. I would have rather he said, "You've only done a few guest spots on TV. Wait till you're a regular on a hit show like me. That's when the women start pouring in!"

Not that I wasn't trying to meet a woman on that set. I'd try to interact with the writer's assistants, stand-ins, script supervisors, and other female crew, eyeing their left hand for rings. I tried to strike up a conversation with one ringless cute production assistant at the craft service table.

"This is a nice set. You like working here?" I asked.

"Yes, it is nice." She smiled politely, but moved on to her co-workers.

I sadly watched them laughing, trading inside jokes and playfully catching up with each other. This is the perennial plight of the guest star that was only beginning to dawn on me. If I had the luxury of being there week after week, I could slowly build up a flirting familiarity with one of them. But I was only there for the week and feared I was coming off like an overeager puppy let out of its kennel.

As on most shows, the crew was very nice, but I knew there was no great point in palling up to me. It's like war, where you don't want to get too close to someone because they might get picked off. And in the guest star's case, your fate is already a foregone conclusion: they knew I'd be gone at the end of the week.

I was nervous about the taping because I didn't have any jokes—just a repeated mantra. But Regalbuto's frustration with my do-or-die resistance ended up being better than any canned one-liners, and the audience loved it. After the episode aired several weeks later, I experienced something new. The next day I showed up at my usual breakfast place, Charlie's in Hollywood's Farmers Market, and the owner, Charlie, was a changed woman. Instead of her usual faceless grunting preparing my one egg over well and rye toast, she seemed overjoyed to see me.

"I can't believe I saw you on *Murphy Brown*!" she exclaimed. "You're always sitting here alone with your head down like something's wrong. I didn't know you were an actor. I guess things *are* okay, then."

It was my first TV recognition. I had arrived. Of course, it would have felt a little better had it not sounded like Charlie clearly imagined that I was a refugee from some halfway house in the area.

Over the next few days several other people also recognized and complimented me. It felt good, but it only lasted about two weeks and then I was just another guy alone with my head down again. At the end of the season, I was invited by the show to attend the annual wrap party. It was not only the first time I had been granted such insider status, but also the first time I had ever been on a show that was still on the air at the end of the season.

One of the sound stages on the Warner Brothers lot had been transformed into a huge banquet hall. When I called to tell my friend Joel, he was really excited. Back during filming, he had been quite disappointed with the show when I told him that *Murphy Brown* didn't have fancy catering on the set. He told me I should complain to them that the guests got better food on *Amen*, but I had different priorities. The caterer for the party was kind enough to give me a menu of the heavenly delicacies so I could go to a pay phone and call Joel at the video store he worked at.

"Chilean sea bass with papaya salsa: snow white, full-flavored from the coast of Chile, perfectly grilled and served with juicy papayas, mild green chilies, and special seasoning."

Joel moaned, "Oh, God."

"Italian stuffed mushrooms filled with homemade spicy Italian sausage."

"Oh, man. That's so good."

"Chilled extra large shrimp, slowly marinated in a lemon pepper sauce, with fresh sage leaves, served on an elegant bed of red-leafed Radicchio Di Treviso."

"Yes, yes, yes!"

I felt like Ratso Rizzo in *Midnight Cowboy*, underdressed at this formal event, practically stuffing shrimp into my pockets to take home for later. I mostly interacted with the other guest star players from that season. That's usually the way it is on most sets: regulars hang with the regulars, guests with the guests, one-day players with one-day players, and extras with extras. I said "Hi, Gabby" to a fellow actor I had worked with on my episode. "It's not Gabby, it's Gibby!" he firmly corrected me. An actor who played a tough landlord in our episode was with his young son. He kept boasting, "I will not permit him to be an actor! He has no choice. He will not live the life that I do." The actor who played a government auditor kept telling me about all the shows he had done and listed dozens of producers who had loved his work.

Out of all the delicious foods, desserts, and beverages, we all seemed to be interested in the same thing: the buffet of hope. We scampered around the soundstage looking for Diane English, the other top producers, and anyone else highly regarded by the show, desiring those tasty morsels of encouragement that our involvement with them would continue far beyond that night.

And I got fed well. All the cast members told me what a great job I had done, including Candice Bergen who was much friendlier and less intimidating without her cordless phone pressed against the side of her face. Diane English said she was leaving *Murphy Brown* to develop other shows. She suggested I could possibly fit into one of them. This was exactly the kind of dessert I was craving. But even though I did end up auditioning for a guest star role in her next show *Love & War,* I didn't get it. I also auditioned for regular roles on some of her other short-lived shows, *Double Rush* and *The Louie Anderson Show*, without success.

11

Vinnie & Bobby

Remember *Vinnie & Bobby*, a spin-off of a spin-off of *Married... with Children*? I bet you don't. And I bet Matt LeBlanc, who starred in it before going on to *Friends*, most likely has forgotten it too, or would like to. But I remember it fondly. It was my longest guest star stint to date; five weeks in a row of work. Out of loyalty to the show's producers, Fox had given the show a seven-episode commitment; yet its only discernible idea was to have female viewers ogle its two male leads.

Vinnie & Bobby were two Chicago construction workers, played by LeBlanc, who was then twenty-four, and another good-looking actor named Robert Torti. Their characters were very stupid and yet irresistible to the ladies. I was brought in for the third episode, after the producers had juggled different guest actors to be *Vinnie & Bobby's* other weird coworkers.

For the first time, I was hired for my looks, or more accurately, my physique. Back in 1992, when this show had its brief summer run, I was thirty pounds thinner than I am now-6'1" and 135 pounds. And I'm sure that's why they ended up keeping me for five episodes. I was a sight gag who appeared to be even thinner when they dressed me in tank tops and sandwiched me between two obese construction workers, played by John Pinette and Ron Taylor, who both probably weighed in at close to 360 each. They used me as a sort of living "Mr. Bill" doll. The two big guys would smash into me or sit on me along with other gags that consisted of me being thrown to the side or leaping headfirst into something.

On the set, LeBlanc had a ball-breaking, locker-room mentality. On several occasions, he'd put his hand around my puny arm and ask if I'd been working out. And he'd repeatedly ask in a mocking way in front of everyone how my jaw was after I had to ice it when one of the huge guys accidentally elbowed me in the face during a rehearsal. But later, he'd ask again how I was doing, and I could see that he really meant it. One time there was a stunt where I had to dive over a group of people and land in the outstretched arms of the big guys. He insisted on doing it first to show me that it was perfectly safe.

But my being tossed around like a rag doll was a small fraction of *Vinnie & Bobby*, a show that was really about how these two characters were the studs the world had never seen. The best way to describe the mood on the set was that it was like the Chippendales. The live audience was packed with adolescent girls who screamed at the top of their lungs any time the studs did anything remotely physical. Just their entrances set the crowd into hysterical woohooing, wolf-whistling, and crying. You can just imagine what happened when one referred to his beautiful hair or made an innuendo suggesting that he might take off an article of clothing. Bobby had his signature seduction piece referred to as "the full Bobby experience." He'd gyrate his hips and point his fingers in the air à la Travolta in *Saturday Night Fever*.

I had joked that since the screaming crowd was such a large part of the show, there should be a camera on them, so they could cut to their reactions. No other sitcom had ever so blatantly broken their reality like that. Someone on the set, for a nanosecond, actually thought that might be a good idea.

The writing was so minimal that a few episodes ended up being shorter than the required twenty-two minutes, so to stretch them out, they had us construction workers just sing at the end. We sang "Ruby Baby" and "Get a Job" to finalize two episodes. I think Matt thought they were cool. Robert Torti came from the Broadway musical *Starlight Express* and he loved to sing. I was embarrassed. The director gave us a note, "Now everyone, really try to sing—except for Fred." They knew I couldn't hold a note.

The wrap party for *Vinnie & Bobby* was at a video arcade. All guests were handed a roll of quarters to go crazy. Pinball was my favorite. There are other games where you can figure out their pattern and lick them. Not so with pinball. I love the mixture of random luck and quick reflexes. I had finally achieved multi-ball on one of my old favorites, "Firepower," when one of the writers came over and gave me the mixed news.

"You know, if the show's picked up, you're going to be a regular."

I had already gotten a hint of this from one of the producers but any excitement lasted less than a second.

"But you also know that that's moot," he added. "This show is deader than any show has ever been."

I knew that too. I can't recall anyone involved with *Vinnie & Bobby* who thought it could land anywhere on Fox's fall schedule. It was dreadfully bad. In 1995, a television book entitled *Bad TV: The Very Best of the Very Worst* was published. Not surprisingly, *Vinnie & Bobby* found a prominent spot. I have a video of my episodes and find it to be actually entertaining in a demented way. LeBlanc was just glad that the contract he had signed was going to pay him for thirteen episodes, when the show only went seven. He told me that when the check came he was going to buy himself another motorcycle. Bikes were his passion.

After *Vinnie & Bobby,* I went from my record five consecutive weeks of working in a row, to another seven months of unemployment, when I found myself at a horrendous cattle call commercial audition. A small waiting room was littered with actors all vying for a shot at some regional ad. The actors were making the same lame jokes you hear on every one of these calls: "Everyone, go home! I got the part! No need for you guys to read for it!" I have no recollection of how the audition went or even what it was for. But I do remember as I was leaving seeing Matt LeBlanc walk in and sign his name on what had to be a fourth piece of paper, each having over twenty-five names on it.

"Hey, how's it going, Matt?" I asked.

He just nodded "hi" to me and walked to the corner of the room to look over the audition material. I understood the look on his face. I didn't feel snubbed at all. Only months before, he was the star hunk of his own show, who had a star dressing room and all the women screaming for him. He was making the big money and I was the geeky guest guy a far distance down the pecking order. And now here we were, both desperately vying for the same local TV ad.

12

CAN I GET MYSELF HIRED AS A REGULAR? "I DON'T THINK SO"

I actually was asked back to *Murphy Brown*, but for a different part. Instead of a jerky usher I was now a jerky deli guy. In the scene I was making a sandwich for the flustered "FYI" anchor, Jim Dial, and not doing what he wanted. Whenever Dial tried to correct what I was doing, I flatly replied, "I don't think so."

I felt like I was finally getting somewhere—two appearances on a longstanding hit show. But a few days after it aired, my mother expertly brought me crashing back to Earth. Usually she starts a conversation by asking: "Anything good happening, or the same?" When I heard her voice on the other end of the phone, I knew any information fed to her would be put through her meat grinder and come out negative on the other end.

"Hi, Ma, did you see me on *Murphy Brown*?" Long pause. Maybe she didn't hear me. "You know, Ma, it's a big show to be on."

"I know that, but it's always so long from one job to the next. How long has it been since your last one?"

"Not so long. Just a little while." I didn't want to admit to her that it had actually been ten months since I had worked on *Vinnie & Bobby*.

"Don't you think it would be better to be a regular on a show?"

This is the kind of expert advice I get all the time, and not just from my mother. "You're so funny, you should be a regular," as if the only thing stopping me is that I hadn't heard of that career path. I suppose people think I could just finish a week on a show and then handcuff myself to the set, or demand political asylum. Maybe that's my whole career problem: when the work is over, I leave too easily.

Between my first two appearances on *Murphy Brown* the show had become a lightning rod in the culture, because in May 1992, Vice President Dan Quayle attacked it for portraying an unwed mother as a hero, saying it was helping erode family values. (Since then, many shows including *Friends* have portrayed similar situations, but at the time it was a novelty.) The controversy had actually made the ratings soar and when the show won the Emmy that year, Diane English thanked Dan Quayle. But apparently, some very enraged Americans agreed with the Vice President and made threats against Candice Bergen's life. It seemed they couldn't make the distinction between the actress and the fictional character who was doing this "terrible thing." During a taping, some nut had charged the stage. He did not get far. They were not sure if this was a result of the controversy, but after that no one was taking any chances.

Security was obviously tighter than the first time I was on. Anytime anyone entered the set, they had to sign in and wear an identification sticker. Candice Bergen now had her own private security guard who never was more than several feet away from her. Again, I didn't have much contact with her. It wasn't worth brushing aside her very stringent private security just to engage in small talk.

My scenes were with Charles Kimbrough, who played the stuffy news anchor Jim Dial. Kimbrough, who had kicked around Broadway for years, was thrilled to be on *Murphy Brown*.

Except for the extra security, there was an upbeat, good feel on the set. All the regulars in conversations with me had used the words "very fortunate" describing the stress-free, great-paying gig that they had. Kimbrough humbly described it as "winning the lottery." There were no prima donnas on that set as far as I could tell.

Diane English had left to create another show, and two former actors-turned-writers, Gary Dontzig and Steven Peterman, had taken over. They were extremely accessible to me. In a show of support on the following weekend, they, along with the other writers, even came to see my act at a little comedy club in West L.A.

But by August 1993, six months had passed, and I hadn't found work. I had read an article about how *Murphy Brown* was bringing in Scott Bakula and some other new characters that season. So I took a shot. I wrote them a letter asking for a meeting because I had an idea for how I, too, could be a new regular character on their show.

At the pay phone one day on Victory and Van Nuys, I beeped in for my messages for the umpteenth time and was surprised to hear that Steve Peterman had responded to my letter. My favorite pastime is beeping in for my answering machine messages. It's amazing how happy it makes me when the machine picks up after just two rings, indicating that there is a message. In the three seconds it takes the machine to rewind and play it back, my fantasy goes everywhere. Maybe this message could be something big that changes my life. Anything is possible. Perhaps it's some job offering. Maybe someone always had me in mind and now has the power to make a movie and wants me in it.

Or maybe it's love. Maybe some woman from the past is available and confesses she always liked me and now she can't contain it any longer.

Or if not something big like that, maybe there's an audition.

Or maybe the message is good feedback. Maybe someone has news that someone likes me and, not now, but at some future point this can lead to something good.

Some days I'll beep in practically every ten minutes, even though most of the time even if there's news, it isn't that pressing. I try hard to wait. The longest I can hold out is a half an hour.

That day, Peterman's message was: "We got your letter and we usually don't take outside suggestions from actors about how they could be on our show, but we, being former actors ourselves, have an understanding, so why don't you just come by during lunch and say 'hi'."

I was torn between thinking I had made some headway, or that the guy just felt sorry for me and was being polite. Now that I think back on this, it's kind of amazing that he responded so kindly. Many producers would likely be offended by some outsider giving them self-serving input. The last thing they want to hear is someone like me telling them, "I know you guys are coming up with story arcs for your season, but I've got a way to go you haven't thought of, better than what you're all coming up with here."

I took him up on the offer of stopping by and I paced outside their office until an assistant came out and told me they were done with their important meeting. I thanked them for letting me drop by and sat down hoping I could blow them away with my idea. I told them that my idea was that I'm this guy that always comes by the office, because I have a crush on Corky (Faith Ford). Each episode I come by with a new personality trying to impress her. Maybe one week I'd be my pathetic version of a cool brooding actor, and one week I'd think I was a tough-as-nails Jeff Bridges type.

When I finished, there was an uncomfortable silence in the room. They just sat there, looking at me like I was a crazy person on a bus, who had just screamed gibberish at them.

I tried to recover. "I'd do funny things thinking I'm impressing her."

That was followed by more uncomfortable silence. My pitch was too vague. I suppose I was hoping that they'd see something in my idea and riff off of it and come up with their own ways I could be on the show.

In essence, I was saying to them, "Please just make me a regular! That's my idea. Find some way to squeeze me in. I'll only take a few seconds of each episode. Come on, you know I'm funny! Me in your show is the idea!"

I tried one last time to save face. "Or maybe once in a while I could pop up, not every episode, just once in a while. You know, I'm like having a crush on her."

One of them shrugged his shoulders. To be nice, and they both were, he might have muttered "I see." They then announced that they had to get back to work.

Trying to break the uncomfortable silence, I started babbling. I told them how grateful I was that they had gotten me a pass to get on to the Warner Brothers lot, because I loved buying Warner Brothers label CDs at the company store that offered a big discount. They seemed relieved that I had changed the uncomfortable subject.

13

AN EMPTY NEST IS BETTER THAN NO NEST

"It's slow. Nothing's going on. I mean, it's dead." When I've attempted to stop by one of the six theatrical agents I've had, trying to stir some activity up, those are the words I almost always hear. Everyone hears them as a matter of fact, and you want to say, "Really? Nothing's going on? Isn't this the land of show business where they make most of the TV shows and movies?"

I remember stepping into my latest agency asking why I hadn't had any auditions. The owner pointed to his computer demonstrating just how dead things were. I didn't ask what that meant, just assumed his computer was completely empty, so I stepped out of his office and into Gloria's, his partner, just to say hi and show my face to her too.

"Can't talk, it's crazy! It's crazy busy!" she exclaimed trying to get rid of me.

"But Mike said it was dead," I wanted to say.

It took me well over a decade to learn that once you've worked a certain amount and people know who you are, there's only so much your agent can do. Most of them just field calls when someone calls for you. Most jobs come from people you've worked for before or people who ask for you. Usually the casting agents or their assistants call up and have in mind the people they think will fit into some certain role for an audition, or with an offer for the part. They're usually in a rush and want to get the type as close to what the producers are looking for.

People will say, "Can't your agent submit you for different kinds of stuff, like killers or detectives in gritty movies?" That might happen if you're an established name like Steve Buscemi, but not in guest guy world. If it's a yuppie who thinks Will Smith is a mugger in *The Fresh Prince of Bel-Air*, or a dock worker who saw something suspicious in *Law & Order*, you got to look like that and not be a distraction.

Most actors think they're missing out on some great opportunities and scour the city looking for that role their agent didn't think of them for. I witnessed some of this desperation back in the early nineties with a new agency that had a box next to its building where actors could pick up their sides and scripts for auditions all hours of the night. (This of course was before the accessibility of getting them so readily and paper-free by e-mail.) There would be a pile of sealed manila envelopes with each actor's name on it. It was a medium-sized agency, there were no marquee names I recognized as I leafed through the stack looking for my envelope. They were mostly character actors. I remember waiting for comedian John Byner to get his packet while I stood by one time.

On one particular night, I found my envelope while another actor I didn't know stood by watching me.

"What's it for?" he asked.

"*Empty Nest*," I told him.

He waved his hand in disgust and shook his head.

"Why aren't I up for that?!" He was about thirty-five, unshaven, and seemed ragged from fretting over his career.

"You like this agency?" he asked.

"They're okay I guess."

"They suck! They tell me it's slow, that there's no auditions. I saw the box. It's jammed with scripts for other people's auditions, but not for me! I'm gonna give it to them tomorrow!"

He stormed off and reminded me that in Hollywood there's always someone to make you feel you've actually got it together, or are less desperate. Only in showbiz could someone like me refer to someone else as a "character." I admit there have been times that I've found my envelope, but continued leafing through out of curiosity to see who else had an audition. But I had never come over to stalk the box when I had no reason to make the trip.

I skimmed through the sides as I was opening my car door. It was the part of a perennial hypochondriac who comes to this clinic every day and runs down a litany of his ailments.

"My eyes are itchy, my throat has a tickle, my stomach is twinging, and I have a ringing in my left ear. Then there's the usual shooting pains, foot sores, post nasal drip, and heart palpitations. But who's complaining?"

That seemed like a pretty good fit for me. Sometimes on the sheet with the information where and when the reading is, they'll also say which producers will be there. I had mixed feelings when I saw that Bob Tischler, my old boss from *Nightlife with David Brenner,* was now running *Empty Nest.* We had not left off on the best of terms. My last days there were not a warm experience. I knew even if it was a good experience, a familiar face in the room isn't always a good thing. I had learned auditioning for someone you had some kind of history with doesn't always mean you have leverage. I have read for friends from my stand-up days and people I've worked for on other shows to no avail. Sometimes old acquaintances can be the toughest rooms. They start off very friendly and when it comes to the reading, they sit there with their arms folded and then quickly thank you for coming by when it's over.

Was I being brought in just so he could taunt me? I pictured him sitting there making me sweat, telling me with his blank stare he still has power over me.

"Oh, this is the guy who thought he didn't have to write topical jokes. I fired you back then and now I can decide if you're working for me or not again."

But what choice did I have? So I went to the audition, and I admit I let paranoia get the best of me. It was a very friendly room. We did some minor catching up before I read. I got some great laughs as the part of Mr. Garrison, the clinic's resident hypochondriac.

The late great comedic actor Richard Mulligan starred as Dr. Harry Weston on that show. The sixth season when I had my appearance, he was working in a clinic in downtown Miami. I was excited that I was referred to in the script as the hypochondriac who's at the clinic every day. I took that, hoping I could return and be a recurring part of the show.

There were some other changes that season besides Dr. Weston moving from private practice to the inner city clinic. Marsha Warfield from *Night Court* and Estelle Getty who reprised her role as Sophia from *The Golden Girls* were brought on. Both obviously were fortunate to go from one nice home to another one. Gone from the show was Kristy McNichol due to her struggle with clinical depression. She played a cop, so that season they only referred to her as being away on "undercover assignment." As far as I could tell, there was no mention of her around the set. The taping seemed to go very smoothly. The only distraction was Bear, the dog who portrayed Dreyfuss, the Weston's family pet. All he had to do was coyly turn his head and nuzzle his face on Carol Weston's (Dinah Manoff) lap. Bear kept messing up. On several takes he'd bark out of place during her lines. And on several other cues he did nothing at all. The audience loved it. His trainer stood by his side, frantically giving the dog cues to get him to respond at the proper time. Bear seemed more concerned with his trainer. He got up out of his chair once and approached him. One of the crew watched with sadness and remarked to me, "The dog's senile. The guy's in denial about it, but Dreyfuss has lost his step."

There was another dog that looked just like Dreyfuss (Bear) in a cage and the trainer was teaching him how to do all the tricks; another young actor waiting to step in. Finally the producers said they had the shot they needed in an earlier taping. Sometimes tricky shots with animals or little kids are filmed earlier during the day if the performer can't do it in front of the live crowd.

The trainer passed with his dog in front of me after their scene. The dog walked on, oblivious that what he just did might affect his showbiz future. But the trainer had an inconsolable look on his face. His head was down. He looked like he was the one walking with his tail between his legs. Trainers take what their animals do very personally. I was not sure if I was watching a sad passing.

Although I was referred to as the guy who came by the clinic every day, there was no indication I'd be back after that. Bob Tischler shook my hand and told me I did a great job. That was a better way to end a job than being told to clean out my office.

14

MURPHY/CLARK

Sometimes the hardest thing about a job is being allowed to do it. I was asked back for a third appearance on *Murphy Brown*. I was relieved that I hadn't alienated the producers with my self-serving character pitch. In fact, my agent told me, the staff was excited to have me back.

Yet when I arrived at the Warner Brothers lot the security guard wouldn't let me in the gate. My name wasn't on the drive-on list. This indignity happens more often than not when you're guest starring and helps rub in your temporary status. For what seems like an eternity, the guard will tap the keys on his computer, trying to find my name. He will shake his head in frustration, as if I had asked him to decode an enemy espionage document.

After a couple of minutes, everyone behind me starts honking their horns and cursing me out, because they too want to make a good impression and be on time. Then, when the guard gives up, I have to pull my car to the side and phone someone on the set to fix the problem. It's just a simple oversight, but while I am on hold several minutes, I feel all the stress and humiliation of being a non-person. Usually by the time the administrators remember to add my name to the daily list in advance, it's the end of the week, and I'm gone anyway.

On my episode, I played a moronic bartender working at an awards ceremony who kept making the wrong drink for Murphy. And, just like with my other appearances, when she challenged me that I was wrong, I replied, "I don't think so." For some reason, though, it didn't feel like it worked as well as the other two times. When I was the usher and the deli guy, those felt more like self-contained scenes. This time the joke relied too heavily on the crowd recalling that I was the "I don't think so" guy from those two other episodes. I hoped the producers wouldn't blame me for the bit not working as well.

It was a tricky situation. After having lobbied them to have me back, it would seem pretty ungrateful to complain about the material. I considered hinting what the "problem" was, but didn't want to risk insulting them. There are many situations where I'm given material that is not that funny, but I can't ever blame anyone and suggest it's the writing.

Because this was my third time back, I felt more familiar with the crew, stand-ins, and writers' assistants. But it still was their home, and I was just passing through. I was more like a friend of a family member, who visits sometimes from out of town. Everyone was cordial, but nothing more.

I did get to socialize more with the cast. I talked with Faith Ford about cruises—Ford had been a "celebrity" passenger on a cruise when she had a small part on the show *thirtysomething*. She was chided for annoying a woman by laughing too hard at dinner. I told her I worked once as a stand-up on a cruise and for the entire trip I had to hide in my cabin from all the passengers who were overly fond of critiquing my act everywhere I went.

There were some small perks to having been around the *Murphy Brown* set so many times. One day I felt particularly excited when I found a deserted bathroom in a production office next to the stage that no one else seemed to know existed. Guest stars usually have to use the big public restrooms. Most guest star actors don't get a dressing room with a bathroom or even a phone in it. And most of these dressing rooms aren't even anywhere near the set. The guest star dressing rooms are so small and far from the stage, there's usually no point to ever spend any time there. It's usually a little hovel with a door that never stays closed and that shakes anytime someone walks past.

On the Warner Brothers lot, the low-end guest cast dressing rooms for scores of shows were cluttered together in a massive bunch. The rows and rows of identical flimsy wooden shacks were sort of the ghetto of the lot. The only way I'd be able to try to find my room would be with the escort of an eager young production assistant. That's why I preferred to hover around the set on my breaks, munching on the tons of candy bars and other goodies by craft services.

Where I was with my life and career, *Murphy Brown* was the closest I had to a home, and that's why I was so thrilled when a few weeks later I got a job on the same lot on the new show *Lois & Clark*. Everyone would be so excited and surprised when I'd stop by the *Murphy Brown* set to say "hi," or so I imagined.

Lois & Clark was an hour-long new version of the Superman classic with an emphasis on romance and a touch of humor thrown in. It was my introduction to a technique my agent and agents-to-be would use with me: pretending that they were responsible for getting you a job. They'd say, "I sent your tape to this new show and got you booked without you even having to audition." That sounded great until I got to the set and the showrunner told me that she'd seen me at a *Murphy Brown* taping and had me in mind for the part of a bellhop.

It was just a one-day job. Lois and Clark were working undercover as a newlywed couple, and I was a nosey bellhop that came by. That morning we rehearsed my two scenes in the hotel. We'd start shooting after lunch. I had my plans. I'd skip lunch at the commissary and head to the *Murphy Brown* stage for my visit. I was psyched! I forgot about the stringent security. The guard was sitting at a desk not even ten feet away from the door on the stage when I entered. He was the one I had signed in with each morning a few weeks earlier.

"Can I help you?" he asked.

I was slightly stunned. I was expecting, "Hey Fred, what brings you back here? This is a surprise."

Instead, I had to say, "Yeah, it's me. I was working here a few weeks ago. Don't you remember?"

"So, what do you want?"

I had to think a second. I said, "I want to visit. I want to say hi to some of the people 'cause I'm working on the lot."

Now, he had to think. He called over the head of security and in front of me they discussed what apparently was an unusual and potentially dangerous situation. (This was way before 9/11.)

Finally, the first guard got his orders. "Okay, you can have a sticker, but don't go on stage 'til they finish with this rehearsal."

I stood around the craft service table and saw Joe Regalbuto and Faith Ford walk toward the set.

"Hey guys!" I said as I approached.

"Fred, what are you doing here?" Joe asked.

"I'm on the lot doing a part on *Lois & Clark*, this new show."

"Oh, that's good," Joe said.

They then wished me luck and walked back toward the set to join their fellow cast-mates.

I don't know why I felt let down. They were nice enough. I'm not even sure what I was expecting. It was pretty unrealistic to expect a massive fuss over me being there and having another job. I guess I was hoping to hear:

"Well, come by and say hi anytime. You're family!"

"Hey, you traitor you, working on another show!"

"Everyone, look who's here! It's Fred!"

Their indifference was not unique. Even my friends and family weren't that excited about my *Lois & Clark* appearance. When I gave a heads-up to Joel, he asked me, "Are you in the beginning, the middle, or toward the end?" In other words, "How much of that crap do I have to watch to see you?" I suppose after suffering through *Vinnie & Bobby*, *Amen*, and *Living Single* (I had two lines as a delivery guy), he only wanted to see what he had to see.

Even my mother didn't see me on *Lois & Clark* because it ran the same time as *Gypsy* with Bette Midler, which my parents just could not miss.

15

DON'T MAKE TROUBLE

I was filming *Good Advice*, a short-lived sitcom, starring Treat Williams and Shelley Long. During a rehearsal, Williams and I were backstage, waiting for our cue. Williams was a charming puppy dog; a ball of energy that couldn't keep still. He was playing a slick, womanizing divorce attorney, and Long starred as a marriage counselor, and in typical sitcom–coincidence style, they had offices on the same floor. He'd try to get new clients, who were going to Long for counseling.

"What actresses do you have crushes on? Who do you like?" he eagerly wanted to know.

"Not so much the typical starlets," I said.

"Who? I probably know 'em. Tell me!"

"You know this actress, Alice Krige?"

"Know her? I worked with her! Yeah, she is sexy! Who else you like?"

"I like this actress Jenny Agutter. She was in *An American Werewolf in London*. Do you know her?"

Just then, I heard the assistant director scream, "Fred, be quiet! You're disturbing our rehearsal with your goddamn chatter back there!"

My heart sank, but before the feeling that my life was over could completely engulf me, Treat stepped onto the set and took all the heat.

"Why are you chewing out Fred? Why do you assume it was him? He wasn't talking. It was me. I was asking him some questions."

He stepped backstage to rejoin me and gave me a reassuring wink as if to say, "I got your back." Wow, how I appreciated it. Not everyone would have done that. I certainly did not want word getting back to the producers that I was being a disruption. It was a small thing, but indicative of the kind of guy Treat was.

Two producers from *Murphy Brown*, Michael Patrick King (who later went on to run *Sex and the City*) and Tom Palmer, had taken over this show, which already had a tumultuous history. *Good Advice* had been put on hold several times due to changes in cast, producers and writers, story lines, and Shelley Long's health problems.

I was offered the part of Paulie, a jerky newsstand guy, who Treat, as a joke, sets up with Shelley on a blind date. Luckily, I didn't have to audition. I had a history with those producers, and they had me in mind when they wrote the part. But when something like that happens, it can get screwed up by the agents. If they know a part is written for you, they immediately want to jack up your salary.

The Screen Actors Guild requires actors with speaking parts to get paid a minimum that's called "scale." If you're not a household name, almost every time an agent asks for more than scale, they get turned down. So when they tell me they're asking for more money, it always alarms me. It reminds me of one of my favorite jokes: These two Jews were lined up against a wall about to be executed by a firing squad. One says to the other, "Maybe we should ask for a blindfold." The other one says, "Murray, don't make trouble."

That's how I feel. Don't make trouble. I'll do it for whatever. I know it's kind of pathetic. I'm afraid I'll get them mad. "Who the hell is he to ask for anything! And I don't care that it's his agent who made that request! Stoller's never working for me again!"

Yeah, don't make trouble. I want it so that every time they think of me, they say, "Now that was effortless, no headache at all! We have got to bring that guy back!" I want the producers to tell their friends, who are producers of other shows, what a great guest I am. "He makes no demands." I make sure never to be late, to always do what I'm told, to never take any wardrobe that doesn't belong to me, and to never flub a line. You've probably seen those blooper shows or outtakes at the end of an episdoe, where a star like Kelsey Grammer messes up his line and then cracks up along with the other stars. When you're a guest cast member, you aren't allowed that kind of hilarity, because it just costs money and reflects on your lack of professionalism.

The stars who make fifty thousand a show and have dressing rooms with the bed and the colossal home entertainment center don't have to be perfect. They're secure. They're on fun, familiar turf. But I'm walking on eggshells. I'm on probation. I'm the guy from the minor league who got called up just for a game and has to hit it out of the park.

Treat Williams and I bonded more than any star I had worked with at that point. He was like my sensitive, big brother that week. He encouraged me to ask him questions about actors he'd worked with and films he had been on. And he was trying to help me with women. He pointed to an assistant prop artist.

"What about her? Want to ask her out?"

"No, they always seem to go for the blue-collar grip guys walking around with gaffer tape and a staple gun attached to their shorts."

I followed him around on breaks excitedly asking him about one of my favorite movies, *Hair*, so imagine my amazement when I witnessed one of my idols break wind in front of me. What an honor. He wouldn't be the last. Passing through so many shows, I never thought I'd be witness to so many greats passing gas in my presence: Peter Boyle, Tony Danza, and Grandma Yetta from

The Nanny. But no one took this to the extreme Jason Lee did when I worked on *My Name Is Earl*. It turned out he had a penchant for constantly farting and stinking up the set and trying to drive the guest actor off his mark. The crew would just shake their heads, annoyed but used to it by the third season when I made my appearance. He enjoyed seeing how long the guest could stand on his mark before fleeing to the end of the set covering his face. It turned out he liked me and he told me I could let some go too if I wanted.

Although Treat Williams was a star on *Good Advice*, he had been quite humbled. In the early eighties he starred in the movies *Hair* and *Prince of the City* among others and was on the cover of *TIME Magazine* along with Elizabeth McGovern and William Hurt as cinema's new major actors. But he claimed that his party days probably stunted that promising career. He told me that he knew *Good Advice* wasn't looking enormously promising, but he was glad to get it at this point in his career. He asked me what I was hoping for in my career.

"I'd love to be in movies. I'd really love that."

"Me too," he said, as he shook his head sadly in agreement. "I'd like that, too." I was glad when he later rebounded with some small movie roles and found a home on *Everwood*. It's nice when nice guys succeed.

Our chemistry translated on-screen; the taping went very well and the producers told me they'd try to get me back as the recurring newsstand guy, if the show made the fall schedule. This was the kind of news I clung to. When *Good Advice* aired that summer, I checked the ratings and reviews as if it were a stock I owned. Unfortunately, after a few tepid reviews and poor ratings, the stock sank rather quickly, drowning my hope along with it.

16

MY *SEINFELD* DAZE

I wasn't going to go to Steve's surprise party at first. I wasn't feeling that social, though I was painfully alone at the time. I do things like that. I'll moan to myself how isolated I am, go outside, see someone I know, and then hide from them. It's not always because this person is the most annoying. Sometimes with some people I just know what the conversation is going to be and I don't have the strength to relive it in real life after experiencing it in my head.

"What's been up, Fred?"

"You know, plugging along. Did a spot on *Murphy Brown* last month. And you?"

It was 1994, and twenty of my fellow stand-up comedians and I were all standing in the dark in our friend Steve's living room in L.A., waiting to surprise him on his thirty-seventh birthday. Like most of the guys in the room, I'd met Steve in 1980 in the New York comedy club scene. Most of us had been pushed out of that scene, which had boomed in the early eighties, peaked by the mid eighties, and busted by the early nineties. It withered for a couple of reasons. One: Television. People didn't need to pay to see comedians at their local bar once it became accessible on every cable show. Two: Demographics. Once the massive baby boom generation grew up and started having families, they stopped going out to clubs. There simply weren't as many people seeking the kind of social activity that comedy clubs provided.

After getting stage time so effortlessly for so many years, it became too difficult to vie for the few remaining venues. Some of us had gone on to attempt lives away from the comedy clubs by pursuing sitcom writing careers. Some had intermittent success. Some had done very nicely. And others were just as in the dark about what to do next as they were standing in that unlit living room.

About an hour after we surprised Steve, Larry David, the co-creator of *Seinfeld*, entered. Knowing Larry, I bet he planned on coming late so he wouldn't have to scream "Surprise!" and feel like a fool.

I was a little nervous seeing him there. I had known David, a stand-up turned *Saturday Night Live* writer also from the New York club scene, and now that *Seinfeld* was a hit, I had written him a letter the previous year asking him to please keep me in mind if there were any acting parts on his show. I didn't feel awkward so much because he hadn't responded, but because I was possibly making *him* feel awkward. I worried that he would think, "Here's another one who has asked me for something and now I have to acknowledge him."

My interactions with him were always awkward. As he revealed years later on his own HBO series *Curb Your Enthusiasm* he's not the most socially adept person. And as I may have mentioned, neither am I. If I'd try to give him a compliment or even just attempt small talk, he'd grumble something and get this suspicious look on his face. One time, I bumped into him at another party where he greeted me by saying, "You don't have to shake my hand," and then he just walked away. As a stand-up, he had the reputation among the other comics as someone who would suddenly storm off stage at the slightest sign of disrespect from the crowd.

But at this party, he was more open to me than I expected. He wanted to know about my dating life. In the past, he had explained to me that I was doomed. "You're a loser. You're a Jew from Brooklyn!" He wanted to know when was the last time I got laid. I glossed over the subject. I said I wanted to have someone tell me that a woman likes me and that by coincidence it's a mutual attraction. He said, "That's never going to happen to you. You're too neurotic!"

He asked what I was doing with my career. I knew I couldn't fake confidence around him. It had been a while since my last job. He asked why I had not written a *Seinfeld* spec script like so many others had. That's why I hadn't, because so many others had. At the time, every aspiring writer was writing a *Seinfeld* spec script, and almost every civilian thought they had a premise for an episode.

You write a spec script to show a sample of your ability. As a general rule, showrunners looking at prospective writers never read scripts for their own show. They know their show so well, they can pick apart an outsider's attempt too easily. I told him it was hard for me to find the incentive to write something I knew would never get made, just so I could have a sample of my writing. He insisted I write a *Seinfeld* script. He stressed several times that nothing would happen, but he would read it.

I went home and thought about it, going back and forth trying to decide whether I should bother. I did have some writing aspirations. I had several notebooks filled with movie ideas, scenes, and situations for myself similar to the bits I had done on *Nightlife with David Brenner*. But I wasn't sure about going the sitcom staff-writing route. Although it had been six years since I had arrived in Hollywood, I still dreamed of making it as a well-known character actor. Being a staff writer seemed like taking on a whole other crapshoot. It could prove very rewarding financially, but the time commitment would leave me no time to do anything else.

Then I thought about all those people who'd do anything for the opportunity I had been given, even though it was one where "Nothing will happen" had been reinforced many times over. I had heard that when Jason Alexander (George) was a guest speaker at a Learning Annex seminar, the place was packed with anxious writers trying to get him to take their *Seinfeld* specs.

I got a copy of a *Seinfeld* script and watched tapes of episodes while looking through old premise books of mine. I came upon an idea I had when a friend told me she wanted to fix me up with a woman who was out of town. Since this woman was away for months, I needed to have a strong image of her to supplement the possibility of this fantasy. I imagined the desperate extreme of needing to know and taking my friend to a police composite artist for an accurate picture of this prospect. I decided that that might make a good story line for George.

And in 1990, I had met a woman in London who I really hit it off with when I did my stand-up act on a Comedy Central show there. I paid for a costly ticket so she could come visit me in L.A., hoping it could actually turn into a real relationship. But when she arrived, she didn't act like the woman I knew in England. It was as if the woman I had met had given her ticket to someone who just looked like her. She got upset when I said or did things unlike the proper way they do it in London. She would cringe whenever I said "What?" instead of "Pardon?" After a few days, she led me to believe that she was going back home, but then I later discovered that she had stayed another few weeks in L.A., off the ticket that I had paid for. That became my Jerry story. I wrote that he keeps seeing her pop up arm in arm with various hunks at all the hot spots of Manhattan.

From start to finish, the whole process of writing the script took close to a month. A week after I sent it, I got a call from Larry David.

"I read your script, and I really like that composite story."

"Really, think you might do it?"

"I don't know. Let me show it to Jerry."

I was quite surprised. I hoped that maybe he'd buy that story line. I wasn't sure how that worked, but I would sell it at any price. A week later, he called again.

"Want to be on staff?"

This time, I was more than surprised. I was dazed. I still had dreams of making it as an actor, but knew it was an opportunity I could not pass up.

"Wow, yeah. I wasn't expecting this. I guess I'll put the acting on hold. But I do have a day in a movie coming up."

It was one of my first and few movie parts. I had auditioned for the role as one of the bad guys chasing Jim Carrey and Jeff Daniels in *Dumb and Dumber*. I didn't get it but was offered a small role as an impatient guy banging on a phone booth. He told me the writing job wouldn't start for a month. *Dumb and Dumber* wouldn't be a conflict.

"Okay. Also I'm starting to make my Screen Actors Guild medical insurance."

The minimum required basic plan was $8,000 back in 1994, and I was finally getting covered.

"You'll make Writers Guild insurance," David said. He was very patient with all my questioning. "It's a better plan," he added.

I told him that I didn't have an agent, but trusted whatever he'd give me. He assured me that he'd give me exactly what he'd give me if I had an agent, so I could save that 10 percent commission.

There was this minimal position given to first-time staffers called "program consultant." The salary was two thousand a week for forty weeks. He had the option to let me go after just thirteen weeks. And at that level, there was no extra compensation if a script I'd written was used. When you get higher up the totem pole, you get $17,000 per script.

All of a sudden, I had fantasies of being a regular person with a real life, having a day job, going on vacations and not having to check my machine every second hoping for that next job. But I knew, even if I pushed aside my acting aspirations, I wasn't in for an easy ride, that the job was a tough environment to survive in. At that time, *Seinfeld* was eating up many comedians and writers each season. Some of these writers went on to do extremely well, but many were struggling even after being on such a well-regarded show.

Word got out about my job, and an agent I didn't know tracked me down to represent me, even though he wouldn't be getting a commission. He claimed he wanted to cultivate a relationship with me. That's how things work in the town: If I had just written my script on my own and circulated it without a connection of some sort, it's unlikely anyone would have signed me and tried to pitch me.

Larry told me to keep a log of my everyday experiences as a source of possible story lines. He thought my day-to-day life lent itself to bizarre misadventures possibly suited for *Seinfeld* premises. One of the first premises I pitched was inspired by a puzzling situation on the set of *Dumb and Dumber*, where there were two wardrobe women. I was equally attracted to both of them and was looking for clues as to which one was available or which one might like me, if she was available. My dilemma: which one should I pursue? If I paid too much attention to the wrong one, I might turn off the right one. No one likes to be asked out as a last resort.

Dumb and Dumber would be my last acting job before my writing career started. My agent didn't seem too heartbroken when I told him I had to put my acting career on hold. In the film, I had to knock on the pay phone where the bad guy (Joe Mental) was doing business with his boss. The film was the directorial debut of the Farrelly Brothers, who told me to improvise, just go on a rant and be pissed that that guy won't get off the phone.

So I paced back and forth. "This is where it all ends, at a pay phone. Great." And then I paced some more. "Sir, did you ever hear of the concept of other people, me being that for the phone, sir?" I am still ignored. "Oh, you got me mad. I almost like that."

Finally, the bad guy punches me out right through the booth. A stuntman, who had been fitted with my clothes by the two women I had crushes on, took my punch.

From that one day of work, I got not only a *Seinfeld* premise, but recognition from diehard *Dumb and Dumber* fans for years to come. I'd later bump into each wardrobe woman separately only to discover that what I thought was a dilemma was a moot point. When I asked Pam if I could call her sometime, she said, "How about you give me your number." Then, when I did get Mary's number, I waited the requisite two days to call her, and am still waiting for her to call me back.

I arrived early my first day to the *Seinfeld* offices on the CBS Radford lot in Studio City. About twelve offices on the upper level of the structure were allotted for its writers, producers, and editor.

I thought you were supposed to dress up. It was summer, and I wore a nice new cotton shirt from Gap, a pair of dress jeans, and a belt. Soon, the other writers made their way up. First was Peter Mehlman, who had been on staff the longest. He was dressed in what he'd usually wear if the temperature was above seventy: a dirty shirt, gym shorts, and sneakers. The other new writers for the start of that '94–'95 season were Marjorie Gross, who I had known from the New York stand-up scene in the early eighties, and Sam Kass, a playwright from New York, starting his first TV gig. Returning for her second season was Carol Leifer, another comic from those old stand-up days. Tom Gammill and Max Pross were a writing team that had worked at *Late Night with David Letterman*, *Saturday Night Live* and *The Simpsons* among many other classic shows. Finally, there was a writer I'll call Perry, a scraggly little guy with a panicked look on his face, who had actually survived the season before. He was nervous even before the season started. The first thing he said to me: "It's going to be rough. Let me tell you, the vacation is over! This is 'Nam, man. It ain't pretty here."

Shortly thereafter, Larry David showed up and then Jerry himself. I had known Jerry from both the New York and L.A. comedy clubs. A few weeks later, two other writers were hired, which made me panic a little. I took it as a message that I wasn't single-handedly making it a great season. A young writing team, right out of college, who had worked on the first few weeks of the brand new

Late Night with Conan O'Brien were hired after getting a shot to pitch some premises that Larry liked. They also hired another writer who had faxed in dozens of ideas the season before. He also worked as a Sinatra impersonator on the weekends and always turned on a white noise machine in his office.

There must have been something about me that made it obvious that I was trying too hard to seem dressed up. Maybe my belt was a little off. I usually don't wear them and perhaps it showed. Maybe it didn't go with my pants or didn't quite fit correctly.

"Nice belt," Jerry commented.

That was all I needed never to wear that belt to work again. All during the course of that first week, Jerry and Larry made a point to ask me, "Where's the belt?"

That first day, we milled about a few minutes in the conference room before Larry assigned everyone offices. In the conference room, we'd eat lunch every day at a long table. Cabinets were stocked with pretzels, cases of Snapple, and cereal, lots of cereal. Grown-up choices like Corn Flakes, but a lot of sugary kiddie stuff like Lucky Charms, Count Chocula, and Cap'n Crunch.

My office was larger than I needed. It had a huge desk with a computer on it and another large wooden desk of drawers behind. There was also a bulletin board and a dry erase board for outlining my stories. They brought in a nice chair for me. It was a big comfortable leather swivel chair with a high neck support. Larry walked past my office and spotted it.

"That's a better chair than mine. How'd you get that chair?" He came in and ogled it.

"Take it. Take the chair. It's yours." I didn't want to make waves and claim in any way that I deserved a better chair than Larry, the co-boss of the whole show. He sat down in it. He sat there for a few moments as if he were recalling the comfort of his own chair and comparing it to mine. After a long pause he shook his head.

"No, I'm keeping my chair." He abruptly got up and left.

There was a brief fifteen-minute meeting, discussing possible story arcs for that year. I made a suggestion or two that I have erased from my memory bank due to the humiliation I felt after getting no reaction at all. Even a shaking of the head or an "I don't think so" would have encouraged me to participate more. No one gave any of my few ideas the possibility of gestating in the room for more than a second. I'd suggest something, and the next person's pitch would practically overlap mine.

We discussed whether George should keep his job as an administrator with the New York Yankees or go back to being unemployed. Larry felt that they had exhausted the George-being-out-of-work theme. A writer from the year before suggested that perhaps George's parents get divorced. Aside from lunches, that meeting was one of maybe five all year where all the writers were gathered in the same room. After that, we were basically all on our own.

"Well, come in when you can and start pitching your ideas," Larry said. Then he shut the door to his office. Right away, he started working on the season premiere and the next few shows all by himself.

To start writing an episode, you had to get approvals on a story premise each for Jerry, George, Elaine, and Kramer. Then you had to get Larry and Jerry to approve how you planned on connecting all four stories together. Back in my office, I composed myself after feeling slighted after not being acknowledged in that first meeting. I told myself that story arcs for the year were not my specialty. I had the notebook that Larry had told me to keep with crazy life experiences and little observations suitable for story ideas. I hoped that when I'd pitch to him alone, it'd be apparent that he hadn't made a mistake bringing me onboard.

On my way to pitch, Perry, the scraggly little nervous guy, stopped me.

"I know the best times to bother them. I'll help you, bro. I'll guide you. I'll tell you when I think they are in good moods. You may have a great idea, but if they're not in a good mood, they'll shoot it down and then that idea is dead for good. I know Larry. I know how to read him."

STORY IDEAS

Composite fantasy.

Jerry flies in a woman from London.

Some guy looks up to George.

The neighbor puts notes everywhere but outside he denies that it is him. Note about answering machine.

The comedian's shrink.

Stays at a hotel because of a mouse.

She doesn't listen. On purpose he starts a story and doesn't finish it to see if she's with him. He tells a joke and she says, "Good for you!"

Six degrees.

Wants to be sick now and get it over with.

Ross, a loser from the past haunts him. Tries to bring him down with him.

George uses the whrilpool and it messes someone else up.

Telling Elaine she is not sweet. crying attempts. The time mom told the "Are you Okay?" story.

Middle act letters.

A woman obviously lies and they are trying to prove that she did.

Her mother only acts like that to her. She's trying to get her to do that. TMJ to.

Got a phony # and called her anyway.

Pet Xmas gifts.

Pretend to be a foreigner to get married.

Someone likes a comedian and also Jerry. How can you like us both or someone likes a group or a film and they are a jerk.

Told a woman he's on a show and then he is bumped. Looks like a liar.

George is scared Elaine doing good means he might fall now.

Looking for Lilian.

The list of premises I brought with me for my first day of work.

At first I was grateful. It would take a while to realize that this "help" was something else. I'd be walking toward Larry and Jerry's office, mustering all my confidence that I had a good idea to pitch, but then he'd see me and shake his head, "Not a good time, bro. You got to wait."

I'd retreat back to my office. There was not much to do until I got the ideas approved, so I'd check my answering machine messages. After that, I'd just sit there not sure what to do. Eventually, I'd pop back out, but Perry would again shake his head. "I would not go in there now. They are very pissed. A very bad time."

Unlike Perry, my interactions with the other writers were merely passing nods of "hello" on the way to the bathroom or for a snack. They were all very cordial but I didn't bond with anyone. Once in a while I'd inform Marjorie Gross and Carol Leifer if I had bumped into a fellow stand-up comic who had sent their regards. The others might have had camaraderie but I honestly wasn't part of it. To me it was like working in a homicide division. Everyone was isolated, working on their own cases, and every once in a while you'd report to the captain (Larry), who would tell you which leads to follow.

Next to our office, Gammill and Pross would sit outside on the *thirtysomething* porch, the exterior set of the house from the ABC hit show. Sometimes I'd run my ideas by them. They would listen, but they, like all the other writers, seemed so busy trying to flesh out their own premises, I didn't want to keep bugging them. But Perry, my "mentor," he made the time for me. Early on, I wondered if that was such a good thing. I desperately needed anyone to whom I could spout my ideas to, but his reactions to my premises and to life in general were not exactly encouraging. He'd say things like, "After forty, that's it for a writer. After forty, we're all through." When I received this dire forecast, he was already a few years over forty and I had about four to go.

He'd barge into my office and ask what I was working on. He'd then rest his chin on his fist and contemplate intently for what seemed minutes at a time.

"I'm very concerned, very concerned about that idea. I don't think that's going to work. I told you this is 'Nam. I barely survived last year. Almost had a nervous breakdown." True, it wasn't the homiest, most nurturing atmosphere, but I quickly realized that a lot of his torture was self-inflicted. "Fifteen hours! I slave fifteen hours to perfect every damn line in my script." I couldn't tell if he was boasting about his work ethic or complaining. On that job, it was insane to agonize that long over a line because almost every line would be changed when the script was handed in and rewritten by Jerry and Larry.

On *Seinfeld*, when all four of your character stories were approved, Larry would give you permission to write up a full script. Then, he'd read it, and if he liked it, tell you to start pitching for a new episode. The doors would close and he and Jerry would rewrite the script. Sometimes just the story line remained, along with just a fraction of the dialogue. What Jerry and Larry did when they took someone else's script and reworked it was different than other sitcoms, on which all of the writers sit around a large table together and punch up or make whatever changes are needed to the script as a group. Many shows even come up with all the show's story lines at what's called "the table." I'm not sure which situation is better. There are some writing jobs that are not too extreme in either direction. I had heard horror stories of what it was like to be at a writer's table sometimes for over ten hours a day for months at a time with a group of aggressive, competitive writers.

The only time we were all together as a group was at the lunch table where we all ate the catered food that was brought in every day. I'd call Joel on my long distance phone card each day to report what goodies I got, afraid I'd get the Powers-That-Be mad I was using my office phone to make long distance calls. I just sat there, not participating much in the lunch conversations. I remember they'd make fun of lame Witt/Thomas shows like *Empty Nest* and *Nurses*. I wanted to say, "Perhaps they're not as innovative as *Seinfeld*, but you could have just as easily written on those shows." I felt only Jerry and Larry had the right to take ownership of *Seinfeld*. We writers were just writing in the voice they had created.

When I had something to pitch I would wait outside Larry and Jerry's office for the door to open. Once inside, it wasn't always a comfortable experience. Sometimes I felt like a pest. I felt as if I were asking to borrow money from my ex-girlfriend's boyfriend. I'd pitch, and many times Jerry and Larry would make disconcerting comments that had nothing to do with my idea.

For instance, Jerry remarked that when I made a pitch, I always hit the same mark on the floor. (Stand-ups appearing on TV always come out and have to stop and stand on a spot where a line of colored tape is marked.)

Larry once stopped me before I could even get a few lines into my pitch to ask about my shirt.

"Where'd you get that shirt? Do people help you? What's the process with someone like you buying a shirt?"

He was too distracted trying to figure how an oddball like me functions to follow what I was proposing. Perhaps he was trying to extract a premise at my expense. Well, if that was one of the reasons I was hired, fine.

My idea about the police composite artist from my spec script wasn't materializing enough for a story at the time. But, they did seem to like the idea I came up with on *Dumb and Dumber*, where George is equally attracted to two women who are always together.

A friend who had had a rocky year two seasons prior to mine at *Seinfeld* told me that coming up with Jerry stories were the hardest. It was easier to come up with George and Kramer stories, because they each had a lot of flaws and neuroses. I was having trouble getting a Jerry story approved, until I got lucky walking around the mall one evening. I bumped into a fellow comedian, who asked me what suit size I wore. I honestly didn't know. He said he had a great Armani suit that didn't fit him anymore because he had "gotten huge" from working out at the gym. He gave me the suit and said all I had to do was take him out for a free meal, and we'd be squared.

I took him to Jerry's Deli, an overpriced deli in Beverly Hills, where he just ordered soup and a soda. It looked like I was going to get off easy until he explained that he was going to "save the meal for another time." I ordered the same thing and the bill came to around twenty bucks. I took him out two more times but it still didn't count as "the meal." I didn't want to seem cheap and say, "You're costing me money. This should be the meal."

It seemed to be a good situation for Jerry, trying to determine how to get rid of this pest, and what, in fact, constitutes "a meal." When is he out of his obligation to this guy? Jerry and Larry liked that idea. I had two story lines approved with two to go.

When the actual season started, and the shows began getting filmed, trying to get Larry and Jerry alone to pitch ideas became even more difficult. They weren't just in their office writing one of their scripts or rewriting someone else's. They'd either be in a casting session, on the floor watching a run-through, in the editing room trying to cut time off an episode, or any number of places having to do with the actual making of the show.

One time, I stood outside their office for over an hour, waiting for the door to open so I could pitch an idea. While I sat there, one of the young, more confident writers just opened the door and went in ahead of me. What fearlessness, I thought. I was Billy Bibbit, the stutterer from *One Flew Over the Cuckoo's Nest* trying to compete with the salesmen from *Glengarry Glen Ross*. So I decided to be strong, opened the door myself, and went in. Before I even got a few words out, the phone rang. They had to take it. My idea would have to wait. I went back outside. I was so mentally exhausted that I walked back to my office, shut my own door, and took a nap.

Once, it seemed that Larry was sympathetic to my plight. He stepped into my office on his way to the editing room. "I see what goes on here," he said. "I see you're not in the clique. I see that."

"No, everyone's nice," I said. "People connect on different levels, I suppose."

He said, "When I wrote for *Saturday Night Live*, my desk was right by the elevator, and I'd see all the other writers going for lunch and not including me. I remember that."

I felt good getting that nice dose of empathy. "I know I'm hard to reach," he said. "But you've got to get aggressive, track me down on the set. Look for a moment and run what you have by me." I took this in. His little pep talk gave me the confidence to not censor myself, to bravely throw out any germ of an idea because I had him right there.

There was a new character on the show that year, Mr. Pitt. He was Elaine's new boss and was a very staunch, meticulous man. And Jerry Stiller played Frank Costanza, George's argumentative father.

"Know what hit me?" I said to Larry one day, taking his advice to get aggressive. "What if Mr. Pitt and George's father had it out? I think they should butt heads because they're both so bull-headed. There might be something funny there."

All of a sudden, his face turned red with rage, as if just suggesting that idea had ruined his show.

"What!? That's not an idea! That's stupid!" he said. Then, he turned around and stormed out of my office.

I felt stupid, excitedly opening up like that and being slammed down. Before I could think of something to say to save face, Larry relented a little. He stopped, turned around, and said, "Okay, I did tell you to try anything out on me. I did say that. Sorry."

Eventually, I did get my Kramer and Elaine stories approved. Both came from personal experiences. A nutty friend of mine back in New York was an extreme minimalist. One summer, he traveled around with all of his possessions, an extra T-shirt, underwear, and his keys in a tennis ball can. He also had his refrigerator removed from his little studio apartment to give himself more space. Whatever foods he brought home he kept outside on his window ledge to keep cold. Throwing out the refrigerator would pass as something Kramer would do. My horrendous experience with the woman I flew in from London became my Elaine story.

SEINFELD
"The Soup"

Jul 26 1994

2.

GEORGE

Make fun. You don't know what it's like! Everytime I see an attractive woman in the street I want to go right up to her and scream, "You've never been lonely! You have no idea!"

ELAINE

Come on, lots of....

GEORGE

Don't give me the beautiful women sit alone on Saturday nights number! That's just something made up by people who work at the sucide hotline.

JERRY

George, she's resorting to flying a guy in from London.

GEORGE

It's different. When attractive people do things like that it's passionate and spontaneous. Any move I make with a woman is desperate.

ELAINE

Flying him in? It's not like I'm paying for his flight.

A writers' assistant patiently showed me how to use the computer software to write my first episode. Before the actual writing, I had to get Larry and Jerry into my office to show them how I was mapping out the whole story. They'd point to my chalkboard and suggest where plot points should occur. "Have the annoying comedian bring over the suit right away. That's too many scenes later," Larry said. After that, it took about two weeks to write it up.

After Larry read my draft, he told me to start pitching for the next script. There was no clue how much he liked it. I was just glad he was going to do it and I didn't want to push the matter.

On tape nights, there was not much for the writers to do except watch. Since *Seinfeld* was more situational and less joke-oriented, there was never much need for punch-ups or rewrites on the floor. Unlike most shows I'd known, after Larry and Jerry had gone over a script, it hardly ever changed during the production week.

Basically, about twelve writers and a few producers stood together in a packed group on the floor watching each scene. After a scene was over, the assistant director would yell out, "Moving on to Jerry's apartment!" or "Moving on to Monk's Diner!" We looked like a bunch of cows herded together slowly making our way to the next set. I felt like a security guard at a big-time sporting event where nothing ever really needs to be protected. All you have to do is watch and pick up your check. But to be on that floor witnessing the creation of some classic television was an experience I'll never forget. The writing was brilliant, but I also learned a lot watching what some of the actors did to get extra laughs where there wasn't even a joke in the script.

I saw Julia Louis-Dreyfus come up with her famous move when she was amazed by something, she would shove Jerry and yell, "Get! Out!" And Michael Richards was one of the best physical comedians I'd ever seen. All of those quirky entrances were meticulously rehearsed. Over and over he would practice different funny ways to open Jerry's door and spill into the room. He also had facial reactions and takes impossible to write. He had a way of stealing scenes. For instance, if he wasn't directly involved in a dialogue, he might make noises or gestures that would call attention to him, and sometimes Larry would have to tone him down. Jason Alexander could sell every line given to him. He had not a vague moment in him. Jason was Larry's alter ego in the show and as a result got some of the best speeches.

But it was also frustrating being on that floor. I wished I could be on a show with a great juicy regular role like Kramer or George. I even saw guest star parts I would have loved to play. There was a part of a pesky clerk, working at an expensive stationary store played by character actor Jerry Levine, who extorts a few dates from Elaine before he agrees to order the top-of-the-line pen her boss had demanded. During the taping, Sam Kass, the writer I came the closest to bonding with because we were both loners, looked at the guy playing the part and then at me.

"You should play that part. I totally see you as that guy."

I just shrugged my shoulders. I knew enough not to pester Larry about appearing on the show. I wanted to prove that I was concentrating on what I was hired to do, to come up with ideas and write them out, but I did long again to be on that curtain call at the end of the show. I did miss that aspect of my former career.

My only contact with the cast members other than Jerry came when I initiated my own small talk. Michael Richards lived just a few miles away from the studio and rode his bike to work each day. One day after a run-through, everyone was surprised to see it was actually raining in Southern California. Richards called after me as I was getting into my car, asking for a ride home. He carried a bowl of soup he had taken from craft services. I drove slowly so he could enjoy the soup he was carefully balancing on his lap. We weren't in the car for more than five seconds when he asked me to turn off my radio. "I don't want to get any subliminal messages," he explained. I didn't have much of a reaction to his request. It made sense to him and that's what seemed to matter.

I enjoyed our brief conversation before we arrived at his house. He told me that he had always done well. Even before *Seinfeld*, he had a run of several short-lived NBC series, but still was able to afford a nice home. I was pretty dismayed realizing how his pre-Kramer career alone was something I hadn't even come anywhere near.

He asked how I was coming along with my script, and I told him I was excited that I had a lot of fun stuff for him to do in it. He nodded approvingly as he said, "Looking forward to it." So was I. But this conversation would come back to haunt me.

It was very exciting to see my show finally produced. It was called "The Soup." Three of the four story lines stayed fairly well intact. The one about George trying to decide which woman to ask out was changed to him blowing it with this woman when he says how much he likes the word "manure." I was okay with that story being changed—by then, I knew that's how TV worked—but my "Vietnam" mentor, Perry, made it look like I was miserable about it. In front of everyone else he kept saying, "It's okay that they did that to you, bro. But you got to stop being so pissed. Man, you're hurtin' over this. Want to go out and talk?" He then looked at the others and shrugged his shoulders as if to say, "Can you believe this guy's moping around like a sad sack here? What a downer."

I didn't want Larry to think that's how I really felt so I took him aside and said, "Look, don't listen to him. I'm really not upset that you re-did one of my story lines. You're Larry David. Who am I to argue with you?" Larry looked at me suspiciously. Perry had put me in a bind and I was upset. I was upset at having to explain that I wasn't upset. I could tell that I wasn't very convincing, so I decided to drop it before I dug myself any deeper.

After years of treacherous auditions, I actually got to be on the other side when they cast my episode. I learned a few things being an observer. Jerry and Larry were two of the best people to audition for that I had ever seen. They laughed heartily after hearing the same material over and over and gave a big thanks to each person when they left. Many actors had their agents call up, positive that their clients got booked because they heard their reaction was so strong. No one nailed any particular beat or line that aced it for them. With most, it was an essence, just a general feeling that Jerry and Larry went for. And I discovered that everyone has trouble leaving the room when it's over. They all do that awkward walk out, practically backwards, as they coyly wave and thank everyone again for seeing them. It's as if they're walking out hoping to get what hardly anyone gets after an audition, a definite "yes" right there on the spot. I vowed to not do that again myself, but it's so hard still to not want to know you got it right there and then.

Five actors came in and auditioned for the role of Kenny Bania, the annoying comedian who argues that soup should count as a meal. They all did well, but Steve Hytner, a former stand-up comic I happened to know from New York brought just the right over-the-top in-your-face element to it.

For the table read of my episode, I got to sit at the end of the table with Larry. I was relieved to see Larry laughing heartily throughout the reading. The other writers and executives also seemed to be enjoying my script. But I was fixated on Michael Richards. After it was over, the 'Nam guy patted me on the back and said, "Awesome reading. Killer, bro!" I headed right to Richards and did something so stupid, I can't believe it.

In my draft, I had Kramer doing lots of physical shticks when he picked up his refrigerator and removed it from his apartment. That didn't make the final version of Jerry and Larry's rewrite. Maybe it was the neurotic part of me that wants to be a hero and have everyone like me. Or maybe it was that crazy irrational part of me that feels bad for people when there's no reason to feel bad for them. Kramer's part was very light in my script. I was nervous that he was pouting. He didn't look happy. I actually felt sorry for this millionaire with two Emmys, who had told me that he's always done well.

I wondered, "Was he mad at me?" I had told him when I drove him home that I had written a great part for him in my episode, but it turned out that that was not the case. I hoped he knew that my version of the script had drastically changed.

When I got to Richards, I explained myself. "Hey, you know in the version I wrote I had you doing lots of physical comedy. I had you stumbling with the refrigerator on your back as you took it down the stairs. I wanted you to have a big part."

I should have had the sense to see what I was doing. I didn't mean any harm. All I was doing was trying to tell him to not be mad at me. But I opened up a can of worms.

"I love doing the physical comedy," he said. Now I felt like I was teasing him, telling him about the great fun physical shtick he could have been doing.

"Could you please ask Larry to put it back? Could you please say something for me? I want to do the physical comedy."

Like a fool, I gave him my word that I would say something. I approached Larry as he headed back to the offices.

"Larry, I was talking to Michael, and he sort of asked me if there was any way we could put physical comedy in the script. I had mentioned that originally there was some stuff with the refrigerator and..."

"What?! What did you do? You don't talk to the actors! Don't you talk to the actors!"

He walked ahead of me, and I shook my head. Any goodwill I might have earned from Larry because of the strong table read had just evaporated.

Back at the office, another writer informed me that Perry had taken him aside and said, "That was the worst table read I have ever heard." He said the script was "awful." I felt disgusted. Even though at that point in the season I knew my nervous mentor wasn't above being so two-faced, I still felt kicked in the stomach. I considered telling him how phony and pathetic he was, but the other writer talked me out of it.

"Look who you're dealing with," he said. "What's the point?"

He was right. My nervous mentor was agonizing over his script, laboring over every line and wasn't close to finishing it. He simply needed to bring me down with him in his fear and misery.

For tape night, my friend Joel flew in from Brooklyn to support me. He was in heaven, no longer having to live vicariously through my long distance descriptions of free meals. He was on the ultimate celebrity cruise buffet. He sat next to Julia Louis-Dreyfus with his second plate of chicken Tuscany and stated, "This is the best meal I've had in months!" To the executives and writers around us, this was not top-of-the-line restaurant food. It was merely adequate. Joel, on the other hand, had been raised on Sizzler and educated by his father about how to get the most from the meal. Joel was also so excited when he visited the set. He approached Larry David, showing him a piece in *TV Guide* about the show. Something about the piece didn't sit right with David who flung the magazine across the room, terrifying my nervous friend.

I was elated that they did my episode. Seeing a *Seinfeld* with "Written by Fred Stoller" in the opening credits has to be the one thing that I've done that has impressed my mother the most. Using one of her favorite malapropos, she told me it was "mind bottling."

At the taping, Hytner scored big as the annoying comedian. When he gives Jerry the suit and says, "And I don't even want anything for it," the crowd erupted. They knew what was to come and couldn't wait. He then shrugs his shoulders and says that if Jerry wants, he could take him out for a meal. The crowd ate it up when, moments later, Hytner calls up Jerry and asks if he could have his meal that same night.

After the taping, some of the other writers congratulated me, and I heard Larry tell Hytner that they had to get him back. (He did return four more times.) As a writer, I was very pleased that a character I had created had made such big impression, but the actor in me was envious. I tried hard to enjoy my day and forget that I was failing miserably, trying to get stories approved for my next script. When the taping was done, I knew the party was over. It was back to swinging and missing again and again. It wasn't that different from acting auditions, but there was one big difference: I was getting a weekly paycheck.

Eventually, they actually approved stories for a second script, but something was amiss. Larry told me to write it up, but he wasn't as involved in helping me plot out the story as he was on "The Soup." He seemed vague. "Yeah. Okay, write it up," is all he said. In my next episode, Jerry works a cruise ship, makes an off-color joke, and then becomes the pariah of the boat. I put George in a situation I had been in back when I did stand-up comedy in New York City. The comedian, Sandra Bernhard, had rejected me. The only problem was: I had never even asked her out. I had found out through Marjorie Gross, a mutual friend, that a journalist from *Rolling Stone*, also named Fred, had been calling Sandra up. Sandra told Marjorie, "Fred Stoller somehow got my number. He said he's going on the road with The Pretenders, and when he gets back, he wants to get together. I'm not really interested." After putting some clues together, the two women laughed when they realized that she had rejected the wrong Fred. Thus, thanks to Marjorie, who thought it was amusing, I found out that if I were ever interested in Sandra Bernhard, I would have been slammed down. I had this happen to George, who, even though he is not attracted to this woman, becomes obsessed with winning her over.

They seemed to like my Kramer story the best. When I was a kid, our family visited an animal resort in Florida called Monkey Jungle. We saw these men throwing rocks at the monkeys. When the guards ran over to stop them, this one guy pointed to the monkeys and said, "Hey, they started it!" So I wrote up a similar situation in which Kramer has a confrontation at the zoo and has to apologize to the monkey.

Larry read the script, but said he wasn't going to do it. He just didn't buy a story about Jerry and Elaine being on a boat. I was puzzled. Why then did he have me spend all that time writing it up?

After scores of other ideas had been rejected, I felt demoralized and invisible even more when one writer was leaving to have dinner with another comedian, and Larry called out right in front of me, "Ask him if he has any premises for our show!"

I'd walk the hallways, go out to play pinball, and stand around on the actual set hoping ideas would hit me. Roaming around once, I overheard Jerry urging Larry to purchase a Porsche. Those were Jerry's favorite cars. Larry actually bought one, but returned it after just one day losing a big chunk of money, telling everyone, "I felt everyone was looking at me saying, 'Who does that bald middle-aged Jew think he is driving that car?'"

I was doing my best to contribute. I also overheard that Carol Leifer was trying to flesh out a story about Kramer making extra money lending himself for police lineups. I suggested she use my original police composite story in her script. I thought I might score big points as a team player when I didn't ask to get a story credit for my contribution. She thanked me, but no one else acknowledged me for the assist. (Years later, when Leifer starred in her own show for the WB called *Alright Already*, I was offered a fun guest part as an annoying cousin who sues her for sexual harassment. I felt that was a fair payoff.)

I had exhausted all my *Seinfeld*-esque life experiences. I dumped out my journals and did everything short of going to a psychic to dig up experiences I might have blocked out. One of the young writers, hardly a year out of college, commented that unlike me, he has to make up stuff because nothing bad ever happened to him. I was stunned. I had never met anyone like that before in my life, a person who claimed that nothing bad ever happened to him. But I'd soon open my eyes and notice that there were other writers like that, too. And they all did very well. He and some of his colleagues were already on their third episode by that point.

So I tried to also make things up. Forget my life. That didn't seem to be working. When I did stand-up, sometimes I would do something called non-jokes, which were non sequiturs that sounded like jokes, but just missed. For instance:

"We were so poor growing up; we could only afford a blue car!"

"My girlfriend talks so much, she has pom-pom's on her phone!"

"She's so fat, when she goes to a nude beach she has to bring a bookmark!"

And in writing these, I had discovered that sometimes by accident I'd actually write one that some friends considered a "real joke." So I decided to write down nonsense ideas as fast as I could. I wrote faster than I could think. I hoped that maybe by accident, here too a real premise might emerge. Here are some I knew well enough not to pitch:

JERRY INSULTS MANUTE BOL.

JERRY PUTS COINS IN HIS CLOSET AND THEY LEAK DOWNSTAIRS.

JERRY DATES A TRAFFIC REPORTER WHO LOVES BEING STUCK IN TRAFFIC.

AT THE PHARMACY THEY WANT TO KNOW HOW JERRY USED EVERY ONE OF HIS BAND-AIDS.

JERRY'S PARTNER IN A CANOE TRIP BY ACCIDENT FILLED THEIR CANTEENS WITH YOO-HOO.

HE COMES UPON AN OLD DIARY AND CAN'T REMEMBER WHO A CERTAIN WOMAN IS.

HE FINDS A KARATE SCHOOL IS USING HIM AS AN EXAMPLE OF A TYPICAL BULLY.

JERRY GOES TO A KNICKS GAME AND AS A RESULT HE IS IN THE BACKGROUND OF A BASKETBALL CARD.

JERRY GETS A ROLODEX FILE DELIVERED AND THEY, BY ACCIDENT, NAIL IT TO THE WALL.

JERRY HAS A PACK OF INDEX CARDS THROWN AT HIM BECAUSE SOMEONE THOUGHT HE SAID HE WASN'T THAT ORGANIZED.

JERRY GETS A BULLETIN BOARD AND FINDS OUT IT'S BETTER TO STICK THINGS ONTO THE OTHER SIDE OF IT!

JERRY GOES OUT WITH A WOMAN WHO WANTS HIM TO HOLD HER BILLY CLUB.

JERRY CROSSES OUT A NAME IN *TV GUIDE* AND THEN THE GUY THAT WROTE THE SHOW IS MAD AT HIM.

JERRY FINDS OUT THAT HIS PLUMBER HAS BEEN SLEEPING IN HIS SINK.

JERRY HAS A CREDIT CARD THAT IS ONLY GOOD FOR BUYING WATER.

JERRY PRETENDS THAT HE IS ON A SEQUESTERED JURY TO AVOID SOMEONE.

HIS HIGH SCHOOL HISTORY TEACHER COMES ACROSS AN OLD TEST OF JERRY'S AND REALIZES JERRY REALLY DIDN'T PASS THE TEST.

JERRY HAS TO PICK WHICH ONE OF HIS YAMAKAS IS HIS FAVORITE.

JERRY GETS INTO A STARING CONTEST WITH A PUPPET.

Three other writers were struggling like me. They may have gone to different desperate measures than writing up non-jokes, but we were all in a slump. So Larry assigned us old orphaned ideas from years past that never found their way into a script. I wrote up these stories along with the monkey story that they still liked. After Larry read the script, he said, "I'm not doing it. Well, no reason to start anything else up. Season's almost over." The other three writers had been told the same thing, including my panicked "mentor."

There were still six weeks to go, six more shows. Did he mean that there was no point in coming in? He didn't say that. He just said don't start anything else up. It was actually similar to an older *Seinfeld* episode where George was not sure if he did or didn't get hired for a job. We didn't talk much about our predicament; the others may have been in too much shock and denial to deal with the humiliation. Some of them were even working on premises for the next season, still hoping they would be asked back. But I sensed all too well that I was gone.

I did want to get my last six checks and didn't want to do anything to aggravate anyone, so I came in. That seemed to be the right thing to do. For the most part, the four of us came in for just table reads, run-throughs, lunches, and tape nights. Larry never asked why we were there. We just didn't say or do anything. I felt disconnected from the show before; now I felt like a ghost. We were the walking dead.

I'd come in at noon, eat lunch, and then go home. I tried to make the most of my time. I tried calling my new writing agent, but he didn't return my calls. Apparently, he was done cultivating me. I tried to work on other ideas for films, sketches, and my own comedy video. I had an idea about how I could package myself and break through to much bigger success. Even though I wasn't doing stand-up comedy anymore, people who remembered me really seemed to like my ThrillSeeker jokes.

I decided to make a video of myself doing lots of those jokes in the context of a song. Even though I can't sing, I fashioned it like Rodney Dangerfield's song, "Rappin' Rodney," how Rodney told a lot of his "no respect" jokes to the beat of a song.

Gary, an old New York friend who always seemed to prefer messing around making music in his room by himself than hanging out at comedy clubs, was going to write the background lyrics and music to the song. Rudy, another misfit comedian I'd hung out with from my early days of stand-up, had the recording equipment.

The song was goofy and rather corny. I recorded lots of Thrill Seeker jokes while the other guys did a great job putting the music down. Someone, who was a fan of mine, got the song to the *Dr. Demento Show*, a long-running radio show that features novelty songs. Then, as a favor, he called up and requested it.

I wrote another video in which I played an inappropriate marriage counselor who had more problems than his clients. I counseled a couple who complained that they only had sex three times a month. I kicked them out exclaiming, "I wish *I* had sex three times a month!" I then asked another couple if they had anyone they could set me up with. I showed the video to some contacts I knew at Comedy Central. Nothing happened but it felt good to express myself. I needed that.

I then started to sneak out to some auditions again. I had called the producers from *Murphy Brown* and told them that I was available. It turned out that they had something for me. The "FYI" crew was down South covering a hurricane and I played an inept clerk at a motel who didn't have any essential items they needed.

I didn't tell Larry I was working, even though I'd miss a run-through and a tape night. I figured they didn't care at that point. It felt very satisfying to act again. The bit went well. I even enjoyed doing that little curtain call at the end. I realized I had missed it a lot. During the curtain call, I bumped into George Shapiro, Jerry's longtime manager and one of the executive producers of *Seinfeld*. He also managed Peter Bonerz, who directed that evening's *Murphy Brown* episode.

"Great job, Fred!" he said, but he didn't say anything about my moonlighting.

A few days later, during lunch at *Seinfeld*, they were discussing possible cliffhangers for their last episode. It was rare to talk about the show all together at lunch like that. Larry was thinking of a cliffhanger in which George gets engaged. I mentioned that they were doing something similar on *Murphy Brown*.

"You seem to know a lot about *Murphy Brown*," Larry said, as he dumped his food into the wastebasket and headed back to his office.

I was busted. George Shapiro must have said something. But what did Larry expect of me? What was I to do those last exiled weeks on *Seinfeld*?

In the last episode of that season, they actually ended up using my monkey premise, when a monkey spits at Kramer. I got a shared story credit with Larry David. On the set, the monkey's trainer started pitching other story lines to me for his other animals. He said he had a chicken that could play the piano and a dog that could fish. I didn't have the heart to tell him that as superb as those ideas sounded, he was pitching to the wrong guy.

On the last day of my contract, I finished emptying my office and said good-bye to Larry and Jerry, who were in the editing room trimming one of the last episodes. I thanked them for bringing me on and hoped I helped and not hurt the show. They said "no problem," but didn't say anything about me coming back. They didn't have to. I had mixed feelings a few weeks later when I got a call from the president of the production company, informing me that I wasn't returning. I felt pleased that he told me but a little sad that Jerry and Larry couldn't that last day. I realized that it must be hard for them to have to do that.

I was truly grateful for the experience though. I had saved some money that would keep me off the road and away from the depressing comedy condos and the unruly crowds screaming, "Show us your dick!" In an attempt to settle down, I fixed up my apartment with nice drapes and a coffee table and got a cat I named Mitchell. I promised Mitchell that I would stay in town to take care of him.

Several people over the years—including that woman armed with my IMDb résumé—have asked why I didn't use my *Seinfeld* credit to get other writing jobs. My overall writing experience on *Seinfeld* had left me feeling confused, numb, and not very confident. On the other hand, the first thing I had done in months that made me feel good was that guest star appearance on *Murphy Brown*. It made me want to devote myself to my acting career and be available for every audition. I also wanted to try to write premises for a show of my own, even though I wasn't quite sure how to make that all happen.

My *Seinfeld* experience had been great for my mother. She was quite sad when it was over. I dreaded the call telling her it was over. I fudged the truth a bit when I said that the job was never intended to extend over forty weeks and that no one else was being brought back. She was a bit stunned, almost as if in a state of shock. It was one of the few times she was at a loss for words.

"Oh, really? Oh, okay I guess," was all she could say. I could tell she was very disappointed.

As it turned out, I got swept up in some guest spots rather quickly that next season. I felt I had to be on the right track, that I was close to that one job that stuck or that breakout film role that would get me to the next level. I didn't know it at the time, but my varied guest tour sitcoms was just beginning.

17

WHERE I LEFT OFF, BUT 20 POUNDS HEAVIER

I'm glad I didn't have too much time to wallow in uncertainty after my puzzling *Seinfeld* writing stint. I was able to rebound at the start of the next season, from writer's unemployment to getting acting work again with a three-line part as a skinny moving man on *Coach*. In the episode, my coworker and I were taking boxes back and forth so fast, it was hard to tell it was me. I wore shorts and a T-shirt, but I didn't look like the stick figure I portrayed a few years earlier on *Vinnie & Bobby*. I had gained almost twenty pounds pigging out in the *Seinfeld* writer's room, and my metabolism finally slowing down.

And just a week later things were really moving along when I found myself on the set of Drew Carey's brand-new show, *The Drew Carey Show*. The assistant director had just brought in the extras to fill up all the cubicles in Drew's office. I was not participating in my usual people-watching when the background artists were put on display for the first time. Something besides the fact I had a decent-sized role was still making me feel good: the wedding ring on my left hand. I couldn't stop staring at it. The sight and feel of that ring on my finger for the first time in my life was such a comfort. It was just a prop, but it put me in a fantasy of calm fulfillment I hadn't experienced in ages. I felt sort of what it must be like to be a regular person. I wasn't desperate Fred on the set looking around to see who I could be with. I was the one with the ring. I, as the character, had someone in my life. That's what I wanted.

There have been women I could have been with, but it had to feel right. I couldn't stay too long with the actress who thought it was passionate to fight. She called me a "pussy" because I signaled when I changed lanes on the six-lane 101 freeway. There was a woman who'd have to drink every night to try to make up for the eight months she couldn't drink because she was on antidepressants. Another was doing a one-woman show where she talked about herself in the third person like a Bogart film-noir guy. We'd be out and she'd rehearse talking out of the side of her mouth. When I took her to a party at a big director's house who was producing many big studio comedies, she took the liberty to leave her photos and résumés scattered around his home in various places she hoped he'd find.

And those were the "catches."

But marital bliss was not in store for Ed, the character I played on the show. He asked Drew to fire him so he could collect unemployment money to have time to be with his new baby. It turned out that the baby was Asian. His wife had cheated on him and he needed his job back. Drew said he'd see what he could do and in the last scene, he tells Mimi that he found another job for Ed in the department store. Wow, I thought, I was back in! And one of the other producers said that maybe I'd be back.

When my episode aired, people who saw it complimented me. They reassured me it looked like I had to be back because I was there in the office. I was excited. The show was taking off and seemed to be a hit. And I was in on it early! The show hadn't even aired before I did my part. As a guest star actor, that's when you have the most hope. You hope you can get in on it on the ground floor and go with it for a run. You can't but hope that since it's early in the inception of the series, they're still playing around with possible characters that are clicking in the show's setting. It happened to Kathy Kinney who played Drew's nemesis, Mimi, the week before I worked on the show. She was doing just a guest spot and they decided to keep her on.

I could tell that it would be a fun set to be on. Drew, true to the character he played, was a regular, working good guy. Sometimes a show will do what they call pickups after the studio audience has been sent home. They may not want to keep the crowd that long for certain scenes where they want to go for different camera angles or try alternate dialogue. I remember that we were there fairly late one night and how Drew apologized to the extras that they had to stay so much longer. And I appreciated that he seemed so annoyed when he heard I had to audition when he recommended me so highly for the role.

But I never did come back. On paper, there were dozens of reasons why myself and many other well-meaning people thought I definitely was returning to that show. But looking back, I did have an uneasy, unsettling feeling when I had to give the prop guy my ring back at the end of the week.

18

CAN'T HURRY CLONES

A few weeks after my appearance on *The Drew Carey Show* I bumped into Drew at the Beverly Connection mall on one of my routine strolls. "Thanks again for having me on your show. I had so much fun," I said, still hopeful I'd be brought back. He was perusing the magazines at Bookstar Books and said he was annoyed by something he just read.

"Know what *Entertainment Weekly* called my show? They called it *Sein-Friends*. That pisses me off."

"That's ridiculous. Your show is nothing like either of them," I assured him.

In 1995, a season after *Friends*' phenomenal first-year success, there was a slew of shows accused of cloning its format, but Drew would prove to have a voice of his own. I had just done a guest star spot on another new show that was also called a copy of *Friends*. *Can't Hurry Love* starred Nancy McKeon, formally from *The Facts of Life*, as a young, tough, working woman looking for Mr. Right. To me, that show was not so much a show about a group of young pals hanging out as in *Friends*. It was more an example of many shows to come: hard-working single women surrounded by about five coworkers where it's never clear what any of them actually do at that office. Tom Palmer, who I had worked with previously on *Murphy Brown* and *Good Advice,* brought me in to read for the part of Sid, the building's muffin/coffee delivery guy. As usual, I wasn't playing the most self-possessed man in the world. All I had to say was, "Here's your order, a decaf and a muffin." And then I had to reassure her that I was certain it was in fact decaf, not caffeinated coffee.

I auditioned and then had to audition again a few days later because one of the producers was resistant while Palmer was pushing heavily for me. I did nothing differently the second time. I don't know how I could have done anything differently with my four lines, but somehow the holdout relented.

"You got a chance of coming back. You're not in the office, but you're in the building," Palmer told me after the taping. I had the office hope with Drew Carey and the building hope in *Can't Hurry Love*. The more neighborhoods, buildings, and hallways I could sprinkle my seeds with, the better.

19

MAXIMUM GUEST STAR EXPOSURE

I was about to drive my friend Joel to the airport after his four-day visit when the phone rang. The casting director from *Seinfeld* wanted to know if I could make it to the set right away for a table read. There was a part for me. I was a bit more than pleasantly surprised.

"Wow, um, sure. How long do I have to get there?"

"We're starting in about twenty minutes."

"I guess I can just about make it." I lived about twenty to thirty minutes away depending on traffic.

"I haven't shaved or anything you know. They know it's last minute?"

"Yes. Just get here as soon as you can."

I hung up and handed Joel thirty bucks for a cab to the airport. I then ran quickly to the bathroom to wet and comb back my hair the best I could on such short notice. I'd later find out that when they were casting my part, no one seemed to fit, and then Larry said, "Fred. Fred could play this."

So many thoughts raced through my head as I maneuvered my '88 Toyota Corolla through the winding hills of the Laurel Canyon Pass as fast as I could. Needless to say, I was thrilled. To be associated with *Seinfeld* as an actor was just as exciting as when they produced my episode. Everyone already knew that this series would be around for ages. There were hits, but *Seinfeld* was a phenomenon.

And I was glad to be thought of again by those guys. I honestly thought that when my contract was up, they'd forget I was ever there. I had no idea that they thought of me as a performer at all. Sometimes at table reads, Larry would ask various writers to read the roles for parts that hadn't been cast, or for guest actors who couldn't make it that day. I was never considered for one of those when I worked there. Usually, those parts went to the writers higher up on the totem pole. There was no money for reading one of those roles. It was just an honor to get to perform at a *Seinfeld* table read. I don't know about them, but I at least wished I were assigned a table read part with the hope that Larry might give me a real part on the show.

I had no clue about what part I'd be reading at that table. A good comedic part on *Seinfeld* was as big a showcase as any even if it were just one or two lines, I honestly didn't care. I was still eager to do it.

I made it to my spot at the table with a few minutes to spare. Jerry teased me about my facial hair.

"You didn't shave. Make sure you shave for the taping."

The director introduced the guest star cast. "And please welcome back to play the part of 'Pete'—Fred Stoller!" I got a hearty round of welcoming applause from the cast and crew, who remembered me from the season before. I felt I was getting a little dose of unexpected redemption.

The episode was called "The Secret Code" because George couldn't trust his fiancée enough to tell her his bank PIN code. Jerry's story involved his foot constantly falling asleep. He stomps it to wake it up and inadvertently causes a fire. Kramer's story line

10/8/95

SEINFELD

"The Secret Code"

#04-0707

CAST

JERRY..JERRY SEINFELD

GEORGE...JASON ALEXANDER

KRAMER...MICHAEL RICHARDS

ELAINE...JULIA LOUIS-DREYFUS

GUEST CAST
(in order of appearance)

SUSAN..HEIDI SWEDBERG

PETE BLACKLOW..................................FRED STOLLER

LEAPIN' LARRY..................................LEWIS ARQUETE

*SECRETARY.......................................

J. PETERMAN....................................JOHN O'HURLEY

ANNOUNCER (V.O.)..................................

MOMMA PETERMAN....................................

DOCTOR..

CAPTAIN..WAYNE TIPPIT

DESOTO..

DISPATCHER (V.O.).................................

*

RELATIVE..

MAN #2..

Cast list before my name was changed from Pete Blacklow to Fred Yerkes.

had him riding the rear of a fire truck. I was playing a sad sack who drives Elaine crazy. She was attracted to me because every time I bump into her, I don't remember her.

Perhaps it helped that I didn't have time to prepare my lines. I might have agonized too much over them. I basically did what I always do. I read the lines as me and hoped for the best.

My first line was in the diner, just passing Jerry and George. "Hey Jerry, hey George."

It wasn't a funny line, but Larry and some others cracked up. They must have realized at that moment that I definitely fit what they were looking for.

After the table read, Michael Richards, hearing me read for the first time, came over and said, "I like what you did. I do that too sometimes, where you hold back." He thought I was making a conscious choice to underplay it. I just nodded. He didn't need to know that I hadn't given it any thought at all.

In the next rewrite, Larry actually changed the character's name to Fred and even seemed to alter it more for my persona. My moping around the office the year before must have made an impression, because he wrote some great lines that fit me rather effortlessly.

For instance, when Jerry says that his foot fell asleep, I comment, "You're lucky, at least you got something to do."

And one of the times I bump into Elaine I say, "I'm depressed. I bought this new shirt. The button fell off. Once the button falls off, that's it. I'll never fix it."

Julia Louis-Dreyfus was very nurturing. She kept reassuring me that I was doing well and gave me a few tips. She told me to pause for laughs, since we weren't taping in front of an audience. There were too many complicated, outdoor scenes and they would get the laughs by screening the entire episode for a live audience before the taping of their next episode.

"You don't want them laughing over one of your lines," she told me.

I took her advice. In the middle of this monologue, I took a long pause anticipating a big laugh. When it was screened in front of a

1972, thirteen years old and no clue how I'd get beyond my Brown Street home in Brooklyn.

1979, first paid gig, $15, The Jade Fountain Chinese restaurant/club, Paramus, New Jersey. Pu Pu platters were served during the show.

Baltimore, Maryland, City Lights, 1981. With comic Dean Rainsburg. They spelled my name wrong, but the thrill of seeing it on a sign the first time!

The perks of being a guest star for a week: the free food they constantly bring out. Backstage, *Everybody Loves Raymond*, 1997.

With fellow character actor David Higgins, my birthday party in 1992.

My prized *King of Queens* Christmas jacket I received, and then had to hunt down from a woman who didn't want to give it back to me.

On the set of *Dumb and Dumber*, 1994. About to get punched for being annoying.

Punched out near the phone booth in *Dumb and Dumber.*

Me and "Barry" the chimp waiting to shoot his scene for the *Seinfeld* episode, "The Face Painter." 1995. Photo credit: Moe Disesso.

With *Raymond* stars Ray Romano and Brad Garett in "The Cult," where I bring Robert into my cult to help him find himself. Photo credit: Tom Caltabaino.

Backstage with Ray Romano, 1997. Photo credit: Tom Caltabaino.

Guest starring on *My Name Is Earl*, 2007, with Jason Lee.

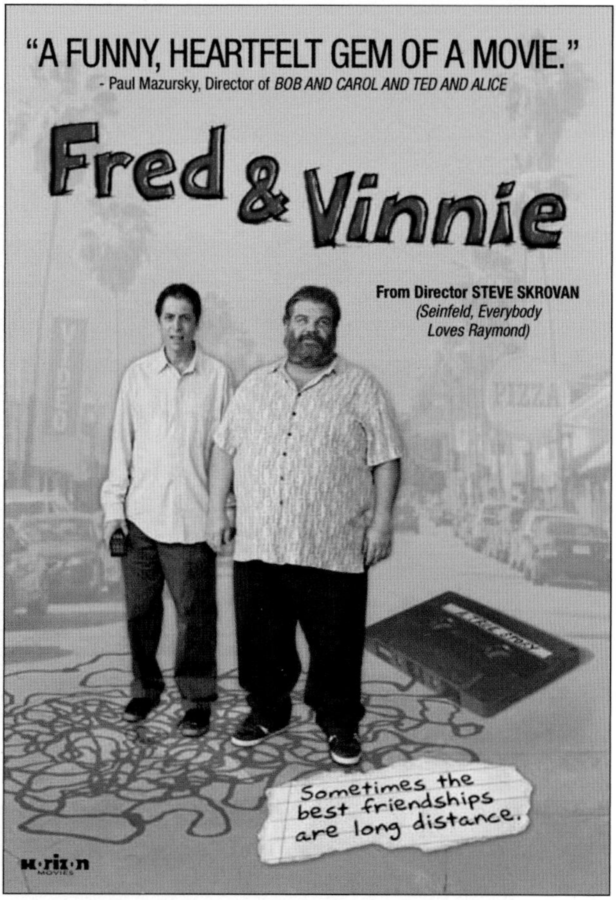

Not the guest star, but the actual star of my film, *Fred & Vinnie*. Photo credit: Robyn Von Swank.

Fred & Vinnie, winner of the audience award Austin Film Festival, 2011.

With Selena Gomez and Jennifer Stone on *Wizards of Waverly Place*, 2010.

Finally a cast regular, *Handy Manny*, left to right: Tom Kenny, myself, Grey DeLisle, Nika Futterman, Kath Soucie, Richard Gitelson, Nancy Truman, Dee Bradley Baker, and sitting, Maria Estrada, 2008.

live audience, there wasn't one, but hopefully it looked like I was taking a brilliant dramatic pause.

Julia couldn't quite put her finger on it, but I reminded her of someone. She asked Larry about me, "Who does he remind you of? Who's he like?"

"I don't know," he said, "the proverbial schmuck I guess."

I couldn't tell at that point how big my part would be when it actually aired. *Seinfeld* was notorious for going as long as fifteen minutes over before it was edited to the allotted twenty-two minute format. When time needs to be cut, it's always the guest actor who gets snipped first. Experience told me that some or maybe most of my scenes were vulnerable. But regardless of the final cut, I knew I had just played the funniest role I'd ever had on a sitcom up to that time, tailor-made for my persona.

For the second time in six months, I thanked Jerry and Larry for the privilege of being part of their classic show. But this time, I was a lot more upbeat and hopeful that the work I had just done would really propel me to something amazing. I couldn't wait.

20

SEINFELD AFTERMATH

One thing I try not to do is get noticed for the wrong reason, but I think that might have been the case with Nancy McKeon. I was back on *Can't Hurry Love*, playing Sid, the coffee-muffin guy. This time my character was supposed to have a big crush on Nancy. I tell her that I wish I could go out with the likes of her, because my girlfriend was such a nag. When my girlfriend shows up, we see that she's a tall, beautiful model.

I joked around off-set that maybe I could end up with this woman the way Michael J. Fox ended up with Tracy Pollan when she was cast as his girlfriend on *Family Ties*.

"Yeah, I remember that," McKeon said. "I was going out with him at the time."

Then she walked away. Normally this would have crushed me, but because I was still happy from coming off of *Seinfeld*, it didn't bother me.

A week after appearing on *Seinfeld* for the first time ever, I flubbed my lines. It was only a two-line part on *Mad About You*, and I bobbled it twice. Ironically the smaller the part, the more difficult it is to nail. Other guest cast actors have described having just one line as jumping onto a merry-go-round in motion and then jumping quickly off.

The director, former comedian David Steinberg, took me aside and asked what my problem was.

"There's no problem," I explained. "I've been doing this for years. I just had a very big part on *Seinfeld* and had no problem. I had four big scenes." (I was trying to seem confident to reassure them I was not a concern, but I think I stuttered when I said, "I had four b-b-big scenes.")

Luckily, my flubs weren't holding up a studio audience. We were filming in a dog park, because there were too many dogs in the scene to shoot it in front of a live crowd.

"What'd you play on *Seinfeld*?" Paul Reiser eagerly wanted to know.

"This guy who never remembers Elaine and that makes her more intrigued by me."

Paul laughed and seemed to appreciate hearing some of the lines and interplay between my character and Elaine. *Seinfeld* was so popular that even some of the crew on the set wanted to hear what was in that upcoming episode. But I was starting to sweat. On *Seinfeld*, my lines were part of an exchange, a back-and-forth that had a flow. Not so here.

On *Mad About You*, I played a wacky dog walker. I had to say, "Hey, remember last week I was talking about dog saliva?"

"Remember? That's why we came back," Jamie (Helen Hunt) replies.

"Well, I used Misha's saliva to cure my athlete's foot. And it actually worked!"

It was hard to concentrate because I had to make sure the dog hit an exact spot for camera coverage as I pass Paul and Jamie.

I felt pressure right off the bat when the animal trainer brought me my dog and told me its history.

"You'll be working with the dog that Geena Davis walked in her Academy-winning performance in *The Accidental Tourist*!"

After my first flub, I got paranoid that maybe the dog knew that he had worked with better and was shaking his head, thinking, "Can you believe this guy?"

Originally, the line was something like, "Misha's ringworm is taking on a tube-like shape." Someone on the set said that Helen Hunt didn't care for that line. That year, her contract gave her a producer credit, enabling her to have say in such matters. Becoming a producer also enabled her to share in the enormous money generated by syndication.

Comedian Gilbert Gottfried also played a dog walker in the episode. At first, Gilbert's performance puzzled me. He seemed very subdued. He wasn't doing his usual trademarked screaming shtick. Then I found out that when he got too loud, he scared the dogs.

Gilbert had one or two more scenes than I did and was upset that he had to cancel a stand-up comedy road job to film. He didn't want to lose that money. I kept explaining that he'd make more from *Mad About You*. Here he was, distressed at having to stay, and I was wishing I could stay there for more than just one day. I knew Gilbert from the New York comedy days. He was notorious for being cheap. When the wardrobe woman said his shoes were fine to wear, he insisted, "No, I want to wear your shoes. What shoes of yours do you have for me to wear?" I didn't ask what his motivation was for pleading to wear their shoes and not his own for his scene. Perhaps he was hoping they'd forget the shoes and he'd walk off with them. And the dog trainer told me Gilbert kept asking for more and more dog treats for the dog he was walking. He suspected he might be pocketing them, though Gilbert didn't own a dog.

When we were done, of course someone said, "Maybe you can be the recurring wacky dog walkers." But alas, Hank Azaria got to be the resident dog walker on the show. Later, he married Helen Hunt as a result of that gig! That could have been me. But I later consoled myself that it wouldn't have worked out anyway. They ended up divorcing.

When my *Seinfeld* episode aired, a few of my lines were trimmed but it still remained a fairly good-sized guest star part. For the first two weeks or so, I was recognized and complimented unlike any other show I had appeared on. Suddenly, I had an influx of auditions. Casting directors would greet me by telling me how much they liked my spot.

The panhandler standing in front of my local 7-Eleven saw me and said, "Hey, you dated Elaine!" Contemporary actors I'd see at auditions and around Hollywood of course had seen it. Two high school students waiting for the bus near Fairfax High School said, "Hey, you're funny." One of them pointed up to the illustrious Hollywood Hills and said to his friend, "He must live up there!" I was tracked down by old campmates from Camp Sequoia and an old English teacher from Kingsborough Community College. My former teacher told me he made a motion to nominate me for the school's wall of fame. (A few months later he called to tell me I had been turned down. That's still my favorite unsolicited rejection.)

I really felt I was headed in the right direction and toward my dreams. I felt I was on the verge of really breaking through as a character actor in a very big way. For a while, I even started getting some work without having to read for it.

The casting director of *Wings* saw me on *Seinfeld* and called my agent immediately to request me. They needed a masochist who was attending a masochists' convention. I don't know what it says that I was the obvious choice for one who craved uncomfortable beds, bad food, and abusive bosses, but I was glad to be on board.

I never bonded with a cast like I did with the cast of *Wings* in just three days of work. In the show, Steven Weber and Timothy Daly portrayed two brothers who were pilots running a one-plane commuter airline on Nantucket Island. The cast got along well except for Crystal Bernard, who played Timothy Daly's wife. She mostly kept to herself. They were also relieved that Thomas Haden Church, who played the airport's mechanic, was gone that year. I heard stories about him throwing others off by changing lines mid-taping to suit his own needs. Steven Weber was a big *Seinfeld* fan. He recited to me the lines I had done just a few weeks before.

I enjoyed hanging out with this very friendly cast, although I had to be on my own for lunch. (It was another show where just the regulars had catered lunches brought to them.) Sometimes it's fun going to different commissaries, though. *Wings* was filmed on the Paramount lot, where they shot *Star Trek*. I enjoyed seeing all of the different characters made up in their alien attire. One afternoon, I sat down at a table with my chicken sandwich and lemonade, feeling quite confident. I might have been eating alone as usual, but I was working! I had a purpose sitting there at that commissary. I felt a bond with my fellow diners, so I went over to make conversation with this woman who had the whole *Star Trek* alien thing going on, silver skull head covered with moon craters.

"So, you're on *Star Trek*, that seems like fun."

Okay, not the wittiest line, but I tried. She grunted dismissively as if to say, "Brilliant observation," and turned away from me. It's not like a woman had never done that to me before, but this had to be my all-time low: rejected by a Klingon. Amy Yasbeck, who portrayed Crystal Bernard's sister, was very comforting. She reassured me that I'd soon meet a very good woman. Of my own species.

I was on a roll. Soon I got cast on *Caroline in the City*, a brand-new show filmed on the CBS Radford lot, where *Seinfeld* and other Thursday night NBC shows filmed. Lea Thompson (Caroline) also welcomed me with the enthusiastic *Seinfeld* validation.

There was an exterior set on the lot made to look like a New York City street that had been designed at *Seinfeld*'s request. Sometimes, on a Thursday night you could see that same block used on *Seinfeld*, *Caroline in the City*, and another show called *The Single Guy*.

I was standing in the alley of one of the exterior sets with a gun, playing an unlikely mugger who robs Caroline after her horrific date. A few *Seinfeld* writers happened to be passing by and saw me rehearsing my scene. One of them commented that it was going to look like the guy from *Seinfeld*, who dated Elaine, snapped and now was mugging people in Manhattan. There might have been some truth to it.

After that, I got a small part in the film *Dear God*. Two of Garry Marshall's assistants told him that he should check out a funny guest star actor from *Seinfeld*. This time I wasn't doing the mugging. I played a concerned passerby, who asked Greg Kinnear if he was okay after he was mugged. But it ended up getting cut.

After one more visit to *Can't Hurry Love*, where apparently I hadn't offended Nancy McKeon, I read for Harry Anderson at *Dave's World,* which proved to be the only glitch in the *Seinfeld* afterglow.

I had always heard Anderson's previous show, *Night Court*, along with *Cheers* mentioned as unpleasant sets to work on. But I had even known Harry Anderson before he hit it big. We had done a club in New Jersey together, and whenever I bumped into him, he'd quote one of my jokes that I'd long forgotten. ("My uncle died and his goldfish flushed him down the toilet.")

I had worked for the producer of his show on five previous occasions. I have never auditioned for a producer I had worked for so many times for such a little part. All I had to do was say something like, "Bring the truck back this way."

I wasn't thrilled about having to audition for this guy, but what the hell. Before I even started, Harry Anderson said in this arrogant way, "I already know how you're going to do this."

I smiled, said something brilliant like, "Oh, yeah." After not getting the part, I wish I had said, "If you know how I'm going to do it, then why did you bring me down here in the first place?"

The *Seinfeld* exposure also gave me the opportunity to audition for a part in the Sean Connery and Nicolas Cage movie, *The Rock*. According to the sides, the character sounded like a feminine hairdresser, cowering in the corner when he saw that he was in a violent situation. "Don't hurt me. I'm just the barber," he said, shivering and crying. It didn't seem like something I could do. A friend convinced me that I should prepare the material and do my best. He said that, true, I probably couldn't play the hairdresser in the cliché way it was written, but my take on it could be pretty interesting.

In the crowded audition waiting area, I noticed that a lot of the other actors looked and carried themselves more like the typical way you'd picture this guy. When it was my turn, I explained to the casting director, who was putting us on film for the producers, that I had prepared a voice, an inflection, which perhaps would be a little different than the typical gay hairdresser. She told me that she would like to hear me do it as myself too, and would record both versions on tape.

The first version I did just as myself. After I finished, she said, "Very good, now do it in your other voice."

I didn't get the part.

Toward the end of the 1996 TV season, I auditioned for several pilots but didn't land any. The activity from *Seinfeld* was starting to slow down.

21

THE BREAKOUT FILM THAT ALMOST BROKE ME

I was beginning to get a bit more than disenchanted with my second agency. I started to think about moving on. I remember standing around for almost forty minutes waiting to ask one of the agents if they had seen me on *Seinfeld*. I wanted to know if they had any ideas how to parlay that into something bigger. At the time, all of the agents had newly acquired headsets. It was hard to tell if they were on the phone or not. I'd enter one of their offices to say hi and they'd shoo me away like I was a filthy pigeon that had just landed on their table while they were trying to eat.

Something was amiss with the agency. New assistants and agents were always coming and going, and I wasn't thrilled with the constant lying about procuring me work that I'd landed without their help. There was a growing seediness about the place. I'm glad I moved to another small agency when I did. A few months after I left, the agency fell apart because the owner had embezzled all of the remaining clients' money. Somehow, this guy avoided jail time.

Right before the agency's demise, one of the agents told me that the producers of the new show *Suddenly Susan* had asked about my availability for a two-part episode. Gary Dontzig and Steven Peterman, the two producers I had worked for several times on *Murphy Brown*, were running the show. I was a bit panicked because there was a conflict. I had just committed to doing a role in an independent film.

"Damn, I'm not available," I glumly told the agent. After agonizing over this missed opportunity for several harrowing moments, I instructed the agent to call them back for more details. I wanted to know if this was something that I just could not miss. Was it going to be a possible recurring role? Was it in the office? Was it being offered without my having to audition?

I had fought so hard to get involved in this little movie like my life had depended on it. I wasn't sure if I could get out of it, or if it was worth it after what I had gone through. I knew someone involved with this independent film who told me about some of the parts that were being cast. Danny Aiello and Sally Kirkland were set to star in this yet-titled film. I was seduced by the part of a mob guy. Back in 1996, when this script came my way, quirky, gritty independent films about hit men were the rage. I fantasized about having the standout role in this cool film that people were lining up at all the art-house theaters to see.

Actually, it wasn't really a mobster movie, just a girl's coming-of-age film. A high school girl gets in trouble when a prank she plays on a guy goes awry and he ends up dead. My character was just in four scenes as the boyfriend of the sister of one of the girls.

When I first read the script, I was ecstatic about the possibility of playing this particular mobster. I felt that I had to do whatever it took to make this happen, because the chances of me playing that sort of role anywhere else were slim. Considering how nervous and meek I am, me playing a gangster would be the most unique cinematic casting in history and, as a result, my career would take off as never before. It wasn't as if I were shaking anyone down or in any dramatic action shots; I was just referred to as that mobster guy. But the words "Gangster!" "Independent Film!" and "Stand-out Part!" blinded me.

But there were a few problems with this small film. The person I knew who was involved said it had such a low budget, all they could afford for the small roles were locals around the Boston area where it was being filmed.

"What a coincidence. I'm going to be around Boston just at that time!"

"Oh, that might help us a little."

"No, I'm no problem. You won't have to fly me there or put me up. I'll already be there visiting friends!"

I lied, of course. I had decided to spend whatever it cost because I pathetically thought that this was my shot. But there were other problems besides flying myself out there and putting myself up. According to the shooting schedule, my four scenes were not going to be shot in a row. They were not even going to be filmed in the same week or two. So, if I still wanted to do this, I had to fly East, work a day, hang out for two weeks, do another day, and then wait another two weeks to do my last scene. Now, I wasn't so sure.

Late July wasn't the best time to be away from Los Angeles for so long. Why couldn't this complicated situation have been in May or June? The sitcom season starts in August and goes until April. From February to April is the bulk of pilot season. If you're someone who mostly lives and dies by the sitcom schedule, the down time from April to August is brutal. I could hope to get into a movie, but those opportunities had been very scarce for me. And not only was I going to miss some opportunities being away, but an actual specific one had come along with *Suddenly Susan*.

After failing to get the movie's producer to change the schedule around so I could be available for that *Suddenly Susan* role, I called back my agent to ask again if I were missing out on an unbelievable opportunity and if I should try hard to extricate myself from my prior commitment. The agent was a little too lax about it. A few days later, after bugging him some more for the details, he finally got back to me and said, "Don't worry about it. They went ahead and cast someone else. You said you weren't available."

"But I could've made myself available if you would've gotten back to me!"

All I could do was hope the part I missed out on wasn't the equivalent of Mimi on *The Drew Carey Show* so I just took the plunge and went ahead with this crazy independent film venture.

It might have not been too much of a hassle if I had places to stay while back East waiting around for my four spread out days of filming. Hotel prices in the New York area are obscenely high. That was out of the question. My friend Joel in Brooklyn was married and lived in a little studio apartment with no room for me. Other friends had moved West. The options weren't good.

I flew into JFK and stayed at a terrible motel right by the airport. In the morning I got a ride from one of the film's production assistants up to the Berkshires in Western Massachusetts where the movie was being filmed.

In my first scene, my character is supposed to kiss and grope his girlfriend right in front of her sister and her sister's friend. None of my guest star parts had ever called for kissing. Suzanne Cryer, who ended up getting a nice three-year stint on the ABC show *Two Guys, a Girl and a Pizza Place*, played my attractive girlfriend.

After our first take, clawing each other all over, I apologized for accidentally touching her breast. She told me I could absolutely touch her anywhere at all. She felt it was most important to stay true to the characters, and these characters were always all over each other. The first-time director, a twenty-three-year-old woman, agreed and called "action." We went back to kissing and touching until she suddenly stopped the scene, annoyed. "What's wrong with you!? Don't touch my hair! It's all set. Touch me anywhere else!"

After that half a day of filming, I flew back to Los Angeles for a few days, then returned East and filmed a scene where all I did was climb out of a limousine. After my wonderful performance descending from that limo, I didn't want to spend the money to fly back home again, so I had to kill time for a few weeks before my final two scenes.

I first tried staying with my parents in Brooklyn. It had been almost three years since I had been back. We were never much of a close holiday family, so killing myself to get back for the holidays had never been an issue. My parents actually probably preferred that I stayed away, because they weren't good with gifts. They were generous, but they didn't know how to pick things out. My mother had gotten a little defensive about it. When I graduated from high school, they took me to the Broadway musical *The Wiz*. During the show, my mother kept saying, "Freddie, isn't the sce-neer-eee beautiful?! Isn't this great!?" People, including me, were telling her to keep it down, but she was very angry that I wasn't into the play. From that day on, she'd say at obligatory holidays, "We don't know what to get you. Remember we took you to the *The Wiz* and you didn't like it? That's it; we tried. Never again."

I came home during another holiday season and again, she kindly said she didn't know what to get me. But I could tell she felt bad not getting me a gift, so as I was leaving she said, "Freddie, take the singles from my pocketbook, that'll be your gift!"

Being back in the house where I grew up felt like no time had passed at all. Just like when I was a kid, my mother had notes plastered everywhere, reminding me what to do and when to do it. There was a note on the kitchen table telling me that there were apples in the refrigerator. She put up a sticky note reminding me to lock the door if I went out. I found a note reminding me to shut the lights off when I left a room. In the refrigerator, there were notes on containers describing the foods inside, including "applesauce," still in the original store-labeled jar. That's because her notes went a bit further. The note on the applesauce told me not only to eat it but when to eat it. She obviously felt that me just knowing it was applesauce wasn't quite enough information.

My mother and I didn't fight. I just found it draining having to tell all the half-truths about why I was there. She kept asking over and over, "How much are you getting? When will this come out?" I knew I couldn't say that I was making no money and flying myself back East twice just to do this little part. I'd take long train rides to Manhattan to see old friends and get away from that house.

22

KRAMER REALITY

To get out of my parents' house during filming, I would have to endure one of the more humiliating experiences of my new *Seinfeld* fame: In exchange for housing, I found myself on a tour bus full of *Seinfeld* nuts, touring sites the show had made famous. It was all Kramer's fault—the real Kramer, Kenny.

Kenny Kramer had heard I was in town. Larry David, co-creator of *Seinfeld*, had lived down the hall from Kenny in New York City and had based the character played by Michael Richards on him. The real Kramer had the same lanky build as the fictional Kramer and the same sort of wild hair. I had only met him a few times hanging out at The Improv, which is why I was surprised when he offered me the extra bedroom in his modern, air-conditioned apartment in Midtown. He lived in Manhattan Plaza, a government subsidized complex for people in the entertainment field. Like the TV character, Kenny Kramer was a crafty fellow who never seemed to have a real job and was able to score this apartment despite having, as far as I knew, little connection to anything close to legitimate entertainment.

An admitted opportunist, he was not as innocent and goofy as the TV character, and I'd soon discover that he had a little bit of an agenda for me. By 1996, he had found a sly way to cash in on the enormous popularity of *Seinfeld*. For thirty-seven dollars, he and a sidekick would take sightseers on a two-hour "Seinfeld Reality" bus tour. Even though the show was filmed in Los Angeles, Kramer would stop at sites in Manhattan where certain scenes supposedly took place. The tour ended at the Upper West Side diner, which had just been used as a stock exterior shot representing the famous Monk's Diner, where Jerry and his friends spent so much time.

He told me right off the bat that he wanted to exploit my writing and acting connection with *Seinfeld*. I wasn't sure what that meant, but figured it couldn't be as exhausting as staying with my parents. All I'd have to do was go on his tour once and answer a few questions on the bus. That seemed worth the free stay in Manhattan.

As soon as I arrived, he videotaped me telling all my stories of working with the *Seinfeld* characters. He milked as much information as he could from me. A constant rotation of cronies came in and out of his apartment, hoping to be part of whatever fringe success Kramer had promised them. A struggling actress and part-time clown showed me the photo from *People* magazine with her standing next to the great "real Kramer." Sitting at his desk was this guy, who worked for free as Kramer's publicity agent. Kramer chided him for not being professional in the way he answered the phone, reminding him about all the movies, TV spots, and merchandising he could be part of if he stuck with the booming company.

"You should do it like Bobby. Listen how Bobby answers the phone."

Bobby was the sidekick on the "reality" tour, a bulky fifty-year-old with a big round face, always smiling, and a little too excited about everything. Being Kramer's bus sidekick was his biggest showbiz break. He helped run the operation, made some money, and got the chance to entertain a captive audience.

On the tour the next day, I had to watch as Bobby ran around the crowded bus for over two hours, trying to keep the tourists excited by screaming out famous lines from *Seinfeld*.

"Everyone, say it together, 'No soup for you!'"

Then he'd point to a bum and say, "Everyone, he is picking his nose. Or as Jerry would say, 'The Pick! The Pick!'"

Bobby had a slight lisp which caused him to spit on me when he led the crowd in a hearty chant of, "Hell-oooo Newman!"

In spite of my distaste for the whole thing, Kramer prodded me to sit in on the tour again. For the second day in a row, I had to hear Bobby scream out all of the catch phrases by all of the same places. I'm sure the tourists were wondering why the *Seinfeld* special guest star was covering his ears.

I just shook my head, amazed that a show as brilliant as *Seinfeld* could be so lamed down. In the gay-dominated Greenwich Village, I had to hear Bobby make everyone scream out, "Not that there's anything wrong with that!" Once wasn't embarrassing enough, so he'd scream it out again like some sort of deranged cheerleader, "Not that there's anything wrong with that!"

Many of the bus riders had seen me on the show and seemed excited that I was on the tour. I was happy to tell them some of my stories before getting on the bus, but once the tour started, I just couldn't hide the pain I was in. I rode with my hands pressed hard against the side of my head to drown out Kramer and Bobby's shtick. I was also agitated because I had arranged to meet my parents and was running late. When the bus stopped at a bakery and Kramer bought everyone black and white cookies, just like the ones that were eaten on the show, I tried to escape. The tourists watched as I pleaded with Kramer to let me go, but he talked me into getting back on. Everyone stared at me as I slinked to the back of the bus. When the tour mercifully ended at Tom's, the real name of the fictional diner, my parents were waiting for me. I apologized for making them wait for over forty minutes, but they seemed to get a kick out of the fact that several tourists were eagerly snapping photos of me with them.

That week, Kramer also found a way of using me for a free meal. In the episode I wrote about Jerry taking the annoying comedian, Kenny Bania, for a free meal, I had named the restaurant Mendy's. As far as I knew, there was no place named Mendy's. I just made it up because I always thought Mendy was a funny name, sort of demented. The late NBA basketball referee, Mendy Rudolph, was the only person I had ever heard of with that name. When a writer handed his draft in to Jerry and Larry, names were always vulnerable to change. I called the annoying comedian Rory Feldman, but for reasons unknown to me, they changed it to Kenny Bania. And for some reason they changed the name of the monkey that got into the altercation with Kramer from Mitchell to Barry. But lo and behold, somehow "Mendy's" prevailed!

As it turned out, there happened to be a kosher restaurant in Manhattan also called Mendy's. Mendy, the owner, also tried to cash in on the show's immense New York popularity. I saw in magazines and on billboards all over town: "Come to Mendy's from *Seinfeld*. Where soup is really a meal." He was being deceptive. Jerry and Bania didn't go to a kosher deli. How could he say that his restaurant was the one they used on *Seinfeld*? At least the Soup Nazi place was based on a real guy and a real soup restaurant.

But Kenny Kramer, master of manipulation, paid a visit to "Mendy from *Seinfeld*" to tell him that he knew the guy who wrote the episode that mentioned his restaurant. Mendy told him to bring me over, and we'd get a free meal. So now, one opportunist was taking advantage of another opportunist.

Add to that a third opportunist: me. I sat in that restaurant with Kramer and Mendy and lied about it being my favorite just so we could get that stupid free meal. What was I going to say? "You idiot, take your ads down. Do you really think Jerry was eating at your restaurant? Does it look anything like your place?!"

No, I couldn't ruin his plans. He had photos of the cast and wanted to have *Seinfeld* theme nights. If you dressed up as one of the characters, soup was free. And Kramer tried to think of ways to merge his shtick with Mendy's. Maybe his tour could make a stop there. Maybe he could host "Mendy's Soup Night."

All week, in addition to being a living attraction on the "*Seinfeld* Reality Tour," as part of the price I paid for freeloading, I also had to hear tons of Kramer's unsolicited advice. He was not shy about reminding me of all my social flaws, how wimpy I was, how I had to be more confident, and how I would never attract a woman if I didn't completely overhaul my personality.

"Are you going to wear a shirt like that if you want a woman? Would you walk so droopy like that? You know, macho is not bullshit."

He took pleasure in preying on my vulnerability. I was beginning to doubt that my investment of time away from L.A. was worth it. I was getting a strange feeling that the independent movie might not be the quirky breakout hit I thought it would be. Reality began to set in. I realized that wearing a flashy red suit and smoking a cigarette in the film wouldn't guarantee anything more for my career than playing the muffin guy in *Can't Hurry Love*. A struggling actor who hung out at Kramer's told me about independent films that he had been involved in with names as big as Danny Aiello, that never saw the light of day.

I was also sad about not being able to last more than my three-day limit with my parents. Not only that, but I found out that the one woman I had ever felt I might get serious about, a musical theater actress named Sandi, was a newlywed and living a few floors above Kramer's. I'd duck in and out of Kramer's apartment, hoping not to bump into her and her husband. I'd walk the streets identifying with the movie I was obsessed with at that time, *The Shawshank Redemption*, the story of a man wrongly convicted of murder; we both were hoping we'd be free one day. But unlike Tim Robbins' character in *Shawshank*, I didn't have to dig a tunnel through Kramer's wall to get away. I managed to get a ride up to Massachusetts. As I thanked him for letting me stay there, Kramer boasted again that he had helped me enormously with all of his life lessons about being a man.

"You think I'm a pain, but you know I'm right. If you stayed here longer, I could help you even more."

I nodded my head in exhausted agreement.

It was fun finally meeting Danny Aiello. I asked him about various New York City character actors and how they got started. And I told him how fascinated I was with his role as the chiropractor/angel in another Tim Robbins film, *Jacob's Ladder*. In it, he helps Robbins' character find peace after living in a maddening Hell in New York City. Aiello was an easy going, good-natured guy who liked to laugh a lot. After the hell I had gone through with the real Kramer in New York, in comparison, Aiello *was* an angel.

We were filming a scene at a fancy restaurant where I, as the mobster, am asking his permission to marry his daughter. He is not sure if he can approve, because he doesn't want to look at my gangster face at every family get-together. We rehearsed the scene a few times, and then on a break, Sally Kirkland told me to step into her dressing room. She shut the door and said she had very important words for me. First, she told me her credentials, and why I should heed her urgent words of advice. Apparently, she taught comedy to Robin Williams and had something to do with Al Pacino getting his part in *The Godfather*.

Then, she told me that I was not portraying a mobster effectively. She couldn't stress enough that my character was Italian, not Jewish. I was being too meek. I was supposed to be a person of power. I tried to explain that that's what I thought would make it, that I was not the cliché mob character. She still stressed that power was power, and I absolutely had to be a man of authority.

When I went back to the set, I was a little more confused when Danny Aiello's assistant agreed with her. He volunteered on his own that he knew many tough guys firsthand and how they carried themselves. The director was so busy with other things, I didn't want to rattle her and come off insecure. We sat back down at the table and Sally kept whispering for me to sit up straight. When I stood up to do my speech, she'd wave her hands to indicate I should amp it up and then reassuringly wink to let me know I was getting it. And I did amp it up. No one else said, "Hey, why are you doing it that way now?" so I felt that maybe she was right.

When I finally did see the rough cut, I looked like I was doing bad acting on purpose. I looked the way a non-actor like Charles Barkley or Rudy Giuliani might play a tough guy in a *Saturday Night Live* sketch, strutting like a spastic, bobbing his head up and down, and speaking like the stereotypical tough guy, "Hey, how you doin'? I is tough!"

There was much fighting after the film was wrapped. Everyone had been nice to me, but apparently, the man who had financed the film was a lawyer who enjoyed suing people and had gotten his money from a settlement after being hit by a car. Among other disputes, his partner, an ex-porno movie actor, had stolen a copy of the film from him. And he had also tried suing the director for being a bad director.

As a favor to the producers, I went to Las Vegas to watch a film festival screening of the film that still was juggling different titles. I had given it my best shot, but in the end, I was beyond not believable as this mob guy. Walking out of the theater, I thought the lawyer/producer had definite grounds to sue me for being a bad actor. As far as I know there's no evidence of this film. I haven't seen it on Netflix. I even have bumped into Sally Kirkland a few times; she doesn't remember me. Maybe that's a good thing.

23

MY NANNY EMMY

I started 1997 off with my final guest-star appearance on *Murphy Brown*, which was my last booking for my second talent agency before their shameful collapse. I had one of those small, off-kilter roles where I had to say words people don't say. It was one of those parts that was so dumb and small it was difficult.

In the episode, Murphy took her young son to a party that had a Martians and Robots theme. I played a guard, dressed as a robot, who wouldn't let her in because she wasn't on the guest list. I had to say lines from the movie *The Day the Earth Stood Still*, "*klaatu barada nikto*."

In rehearsal I kept mispronouncing them. Losing her patience with me, Candice Bergen said, "Say them phonetically, like they're spelled." I thought, "Like they're spelled? These are alien, made-up words. They aren't spelled like anything."

Almost six months later I finally got my next booking. I didn't have to audition. *The Nanny* needed an annoying, moronic pharmacist, and someone in the office suggested me. I had no idea that guest star appearance would be such a source of arriving in the big time. The pharmacist I played embarrasses Fran Drescher by announcing her symptoms over the store loudspeaker. We had some fun interplay when I yell out that she has head lice and she tries to shush me up.

That season Fran chose to not film in front of studio audiences. Some on the set had said that it was because she had just broken up with her husband, who ran the show with her, and she didn't want the crowd asking her questions about the breakup.

The other cast members all were kind. Benjamin Salisbury, who played the oldest of the kids, came up to me and asked if I wanted to be included in the Academy Awards pool coming up. He then awkwardly realized a moment later that I would not be around the following week if I should win. He stumbled uncomfortably and then figured out that a production assistant could send me the money.

Fran was very complimentary toward me. After the episode aired, she sent me a nice personal note, telling me what a great job I did. At the time, some writers joked to me that if more ailments came up, they'd try to bring me back. And surprisingly, that did end up happening. The next season, I returned when she had a rash, and I embarrassed her about how gross it looked. The season after that, I loudly told her when to have sex when she bought hormone pills trying to get pregnant.

Several months later, I chose to skip sitting at home to watch the 1997 Emmy Awards. Instead, I opted to take advantage of what I hoped would be an empty city and eat at a nice restaurant and not feel self-conscious about eating alone, or perhaps see a movie in an empty theater. It was my way of rebelling, going against the norm.

The first restaurant I went to was in fact, empty. Still, the waiter brought it to my attention that I was alone by insisting that I move from my table because it was for four or more customers only.

"Okay, well, I'll come back for this table with three of my friends," I said, and walked out the door.

My desire for the nice dining experience by myself was ruined for that night, so I settled for pizza at the mall's food court instead. When I got home, I noticed that there were six messages on my answering machine. The first was from a peripheral friend.

"Hey, Fred, saw you on the Emmys! Way to go." And strangely, the other five also congratulated me for my Emmy appearance. My what?! I called back the first person to see what the hell this was about.

It turned out that Fran Drescher had been nominated for best actress in a comedy that year. When her name was announced, they showed a clip of her and me at the pharmacy. This felt like a private victory. One of those little utility parts I had been playing had received a nice, small dose of recognition. There is in fact an Emmy award for guest actor, but almost always those nominations go to celebrities such as Brad Pitt in *Friends*, Michael Douglas in *Will and Grace*, or Mel Brooks in *Mad About You*. But my jerky, four-line pharmacist had snuck his way into TV's biggest night to be seen by millions. For those few moments, a guy who had been hiding in empty restaurants for so long had inadvertently crashed the big party. I knew it wasn't normal to have this secondhand sense of pride, but I was beaming nevertheless, although I wished Fran Drescher had won. Around fifteen years later Fran brought me back to her new TV Land show *Happily Divorced* to play an annoying waiter. I had those Emmy dreams all over again.

The Nanny

January 8, 1998

Dear Fred,

What a wonderful character actor you are! It was a real pleasure having you back on the show. Everyone thought you did a fantastically funny job.

We'll look forward to the next time. Good luck, God bless and think peace

Best wishes,

Fran Drescher

24

SUDDENLY GAY

I was finally getting married, but my mother would not be proud. I already knew she was adamantly adverse to who I was seeing. Actually my wedding was to be on another guest appearance, but it still didn't sit well with her.

At the table reading for the Brooke Shields series *Suddenly Susan* the director began by introducing the guest and recurring cast. "And welcome back, again playing our beloved office mail guy, Pete—Bill Stevenson." Everyone applauded and laughed just thinking of the goofy work Bill had done on his previous appearances.

I was certain that "Pete" was the role that I had missed out on when I was away working on that independent movie that never got released. He had done four episodes the first season as the monotone office mail guy and a few already that season. I have to admit that he really fit the part and I was surprised they didn't use him more.

In *Suddenly Susan*, Brooke Shields starred as a woman looking for love while working at a San Francisco magazine. In the second season, they realized that there were no gay characters on the show that took place in the country's heaviest gay-populated city. So they decided that Pete, the mail guy, was gay all of a sudden. And I was brought in to play his lover. Pete was trying to get me jealous and told me that he had a thing going on with one of the regulars, Judd Nelson. The whole episode was built on the tension that this unseen lover was going to come over and kick Judd Nelson's ass. Then wimpy me appears, makes a scene, threatens Judd, and leaves. The crowd seemed to get a big kick out of it.

My week of work on *Suddenly Susan* was not as pleasant as it could have been. It wasn't the cast, they were all very accessible. Okay, the women didn't really eat lunch with us in the commissary. Brooke Shields and Kathy Griffin would nibble on something they brought in and use lunch to rush off to the Warner Brothers gym next to the set. And the producers were great. Steven Peterman and Gary Donzing, who I had previously worked with on *Murphy Brown,* brought me in for that week of work without making me read for the role. No job can get off to a better start than that. My week was marred by myself.

I began obsessing that Bill's role was the one I could have had if it wasn't for bad timing and anxiousness. He looked so happy to be there. It was obvious the show needed the bizarre jolt that he provided when he wheeled his mail cart into the gang's workspace. It was clear he'd be coming back a lot. I was pleased for him, but just couldn't stop thinking about how that could have been me. Weeks later, I felt like a fool for not enjoying my time there by dwelling on what might have been. Then, typically of me, I wasted more time obsessing about how I shouldn't have obsessed.

After the episode aired, I talked to my parents on the phone. They never fail to amaze me with their reactions to my work. I spoke to my father first. It was the usual one-word conversation between us. They had just moved to a retirement community in Florida. "So, Dad, you like the retirement community?"

"Painting class."

"Huh? What do you mean, painting class, Dad?"

"I take a painting class."

I thought it was strange for him not to mention the show. It was a decent-sized role. One scene, but it was a big scene. So I brought it up.

"Dad, did you see me on *Suddenly Susan*?"

He was flustered. He laughed nervously, "Freddie, I don't know. Let's talk about something else."

"Why can't we talk about this? What's the problem?"

He couldn't deal with it and put my mother on. I asked her what she thought and she said, "You were a gay! Freddie, you were a gay."

I'm sure my parents thought I might be gay. Year after year they would ask if I was seeing someone. Sometimes, I used to lie and say I was, but I think they knew when I was making it up. I don't know why they were so shocked. Maybe it was because it was around the same time Ellen DeGeneres came out of the closet by announcing that her character on her show was gay. Maybe they thought that's what I was doing. As if I had the power to say, "I'm gay, so now I am going to play someone gay."

Maybe because I always played schnooks, they thought actors are who they play. I was honestly a bit annoyed that they were so put off by it. But in a way, they probably would rather I was gay than whatever it is I am. In their retirement community in Florida, my father takes many crafts courses, but my mother has no hobbies. Once in a while she goes to a lecture. One time she went to a lecture about Frank Sinatra and on another occasion, before my appearance on *Suddenly Susan*, she took a course on homosexuality. At least if I were gay, it would give me a label.

I don't know why trying to click with a woman is more elusive than trying to find that steady home in show business. They might even be connected. In show business, either I'm all over the place or in no place at all. And maybe I carry myself like this lost dizzy guy waiting to leap onto another short merry-go-round ride. But it's always been hard for me, showbiz or relationships. I've always been a little off.

Maybe the truth is I'm not cut out to be in a steady relationship with a woman. It's not my field. Maybe I've been blessed in some other way to make up for that. Perhaps my whole life I've been blessed with the gift of being the best scuba diver or the best at fixing rulers and have had no idea.

After I hung up the phone with my parents that day I felt a little sad because their reaction to my *Suddenly Susan* role made me question my life. I then wondered: What if I got what I wished for? What if the producers did find ways to bring me back on? Would that only subject me to more of my parents' scorn? Would a good thing be turned into a headache? Maybe so. That's what my mother's best at.

A few months later came the dreaded wedding scene. It was actually going to be a double wedding. Vicki (Kathy Griffin), Susan's kooky coworker and sidekick, would also be marrying her boyfriend in the same ceremony.

Joan Rivers played Kathy Griffin's mother, and I expected her to be a bitchy prima donna. Though I had liked her when I was a kid and liked her book, *Still Talking*, about her comeback after her failed Fox show and the suicide of her husband, she was mostly known now for her snippy red carpet remarks. I expected a pampered whiny woman. But I was wrong. When I told Joan that my mother was unhappy that I was portraying "a gay," she demanded to have her phone number. She took out her cell phone and wanted to call her right there on the spot and talk sense to her. She wanted to tell her how proud she should be of me and how silly she was being. My mother would have been so thrilled to get a call from Joan Rivers. Sadly, I didn't have her number memorized, nor did I have a cell phone at the time it was programmed into.

Instead, the person I had problems with on set was Kathy Griffin. After rehearsals, she'd come up to me and say, "Me and Brooke see you and Bill aren't holding hands. You're being so homophobic. You should be holding his hand more."

I couldn't believe it. I knew this wasn't an issue at all with Brooke Shields. Kathy was implicating her just to be more of a pain in the ass. It was like when my mother used to say to me, "You're so fresh, even Aunt Faye says you're fresh, even your father says that, even . . ."

I wasted several moments of my time defending myself. "Of course we were holding hands. We're slow dancing. You have to hold hands when you slow dance."

"No, you weren't holding his hand. You let it go."

I was amazed. She had to be making about thirty grand a show and she had nothing better to do than watch the guest actors to make sure they were being as gay as they should be. But she kept looking at me. "Hold his hand!" she'd yell across the stage in front of everyone. "I am," I'd say, showing my grip around my partner's hand. "Give me a break, will you?" I said as I walked away.

I had enough of her. We actually had two dates just a few years before that. She seemed to have gone out of her way to make me miserable on our dates, and also found ways to keep battering me on *Suddenly Susan*.

Back in 1992, after doing my best to socialize at a crowded party spilling with scores of comedians and comedy writers, I did what I usually do, being chronically socially awkward: I looked for the host's pets to connect with. They were hiding, so the next best thing was to stare at photos of the cat that were stuck to the refrigerator. After a few minutes, this redheaded woman asked who I was. I was actually excited to meet her in person because I had just seen her as a dancer in a comedic parody, *Madonna: Truth or Dare*, on Comedy Central and remembered thinking she was cute. After some small talk I don't recall, Kathy Griffin asked me to drive her to her car where she made it easy for me to make out with her. The next night I showed up at her apartment for a date. We stood there not even two minutes deciding what we should do, when she announced, "I'm wet."

Hearing that made it seem appropriate to make a pass at that moment. I suppose I wasn't that good in bed, because after we slept together, she kept pestering me to allow her to hit me in the face. Apparently she had just seen a TV movie about a woman who battered her husband, which gave her a craving to do the same.

"Why do you want to do that?" I asked.

"I have hostility towards men. They rape, watch porn, and go to strip clubs."

"I only do two out of three of those," I said, trying to lighten the mood. I thought I diffused the tension. We lay together peacefully for a few moments until she yelled, "Stop looking at my ass!"

We had just one date a few days after that. It happened to be my birthday. We were at a restaurant with about five of my friends and she refused to engage with any of them. She sat bored, exclaiming, "Why am I here? I usually hang out with cool people like Ben Stiller!" As her lover I'd failed, and now, I wasn't gay enough for her either.

My visits to *Suddenly Susan* were enlivened by other celebrity guest stars. I got to commiserate with Tommy Smothers about what it was like to feel second-best to your older sibling. When I was a kid, I would ask my older sister why she got a middle name and I didn't. I also felt slighted that there were dozens more baby photos of her than of me. "Don't give me your *Smothers Brothers* crap!" she'd say. She was referring to their classic bit: "Mom always liked you best."

The week Dr. Joyce Brothers guested on *Suddenly Susan*, I'd just had an unhealthy fling with an old girlfriend from New York City who happened to be in L.A. for a short visit, which stirred up a lot of old bad feelings. On a break from filming scenes, I went over to Dr. Brothers and started to talk to her about my feelings.

"I've been depressed. When I'm depressed, when I get really depressed, I can't eat. I haven't been able to eat more than a banana for a few days. Is that common?"

"Sometimes people go the other extreme. They can eat too much when they're depressed."

"Oh, really?"

"Yes, that is true."

And that was it. I walked away and stopped pandering for free therapy because I realized it was kind of crazy—she was like a cartoon character of a therapist, a punch line. In fact the show was using her as a joke. In the plot, one of the regulars goes to a costume party dressed up as Dr. Brothers and the joke was that the costume looked amazingly lifelike—the cast member dubbed his voice in synch as she moved her mouth. Asking her advice seemed like asking Will Ferrell playing President Bush on *Saturday Night Live* if he could help you get a bill passed.

Suddenly Susan was actually nominated for a GLAAD (Gay and Lesbian Alliance Against Defamation) award for its positive portrayal of homosexuals. It was a little ahead of its time before the explosion of gays on sitcoms. What Bill and I did was different than the usually flashy flamboyant way gays were portrayed. I played it the only way I play anything. I held back. I was pleased it got that little bit of recognition.

But we lost to Ellen DeGeneres.

A short while later, someone at Ruffles Potato Chips liked me and wanted me to be in a commercial playing Kathy Griffin's boyfriend. However, my agent informed me that Kathy nixed me from the role, because she wanted someone "more macho" playing her boyfriend.

25

WHY DOESN'T RAYMOND LOVE ME?

I learned a brutal lesson after my first *Everybody Loves Raymond* appearance: call the show's production office to make sure you weren't cut from the episode before having an embarrassing "I'm on TV" get-together with your buddies, and especially before telling any family members.

After a rocky start because of a bad Friday night time slot, *Everybody Loves Raymond* started to slowly take off thanks to rave reviews and viewer word-of-mouth. Ray and I had crossed paths only a few times on the New York comedy club scene. We were regulars at different clubs and I was heading out to L.A. when he was emerging. But I had heard that several people referred to him as a more normal and healthier-looking Fred Stoller. There have been others that have mistaken us for one another, but I never heard about it so much until Ray's show.

I was warned about the *Everybody Loves Raymond* conspiracy against me in the early stages of the series by Perry, my old *Seinfeld* war "comrade." I bumped into him at Koo Koo Roo, one of my favorite fast-food chicken restaurants. Perry was disheveled with a wild bushy beard, looking like a crazy street person. He came over to me and shook his head sadly. He closed his eyes a moment and could barely look at me.

"Sorry, bro. Sorry what happened to you."

"What are you talking about?"

"Have you seen Ray's show?! He totally is doing you! He looks like you and he has all of your inflections. What are you going to do about it?"

Perry smirked. "I know that sucks that he did that. I know you hate him." It's as if he wanted me to curse out Ray Romano. "Yeah, that bastard does piss me off. How dare he, knowing very well that we look and sound similar, become very big and get his own TV series! He easily could have pursued another career, but no, he did it all to mess me up."

Many other people seemed to think our similarities were a good thing and would ask why I wasn't on *Everybody Loves Raymond*. Usually, someone would grill me, demanding a reason why I was not on this show for which I was so right. "I don't know. It just hasn't happened yet" is all I could tell them. But they'd keep pressing, "You should. You really should be on the show."

When I did get my shot at a guest star appearance on *Raymond*, I was relieved that finally all of these suspicious people would stop thinking I was somehow holding out.

I had first auditioned for the role of a schmucky guy at Ray's high school reunion. At the audition were Ray, Lew Schneider, a former stand-up comic and one of the writers, and Phil Rosenthal, the show's creator. Before I read, the four of us had a few moments of small talk.

As I was talking, Phil and Lew laughed when they noticed that I pronounced some words similarly to Ray and had lots of the same inflections. For instance, we both pronounced the word "now" as "neow." I didn't get that part, but I heard that if there ever were a story for Ray's cousin, that role would be mine. I suppose all those people that said I absolutely had to appear on *Everybody Loves Raymond* weren't so off after all.

Almost a year and a half later, I got booked to play Ray's cousin Gerard. The episode was a flashback recreation of Ray and Debra's wedding. Ray's mother Marie (Doris Roberts) owed her sister a favor and persuaded Ray to let me play my accordion at his wedding. Brad Garrett, who played Ray's less-pampered brother Robert, played up a similar relationship off the set. Brad would kid about how Ray was the whole show and how he was a distant afterthought. If Ray came onto the set a few minutes late, Brad would joke, "Oh, it's okay. Ray's late. It's all about Raymond. Where were you, counting your money again?" He made lots of jokes about Ray's wallet. If Ray stumbled, Brad would say, "It's okay, he landed on his wallet." Or "Ray needs a forklift to carry his wallet now." Once an alarm sounded and Brad commented, "Ray's wallet set off the sprinkler system."

I didn't quite understand that one. But that was Brad's style. I suppose he felt if the gag had the word "wallet" in it and was spouted out quickly, no one would question the logic. It's always an awkward feeling being on a set and hearing the regulars joke, complain, or talk in any way about their salary or another of their co-regulars' right in front of you. I guess it would have been out of line for me to rib Garrett about his $300,000 an episode salary the whole week I was guesting.

Hearing the series regulars discuss their salaries in front of me was not unique in my guest star travels. I had made three appearances on the NBC series *The Naked Truth* during its third and last chaotic season. By then, it had had its third cast change. When I arrived, three of the original cast members weren't hanging out with the four newest members. There was resentment. I was told that the very first day; Téa Leoni and the other two original cast members set the tone by completely snubbing the four new ones.

Comic-actor Chris Elliott was among the newer members dreading his time on the show. On all my appearances, he had invited me to retreat on all breaks to hang out at the dressing room with him and the other guys I had bonded with. This bond came to an end when a newcomer decided it would be fun if they all confessed how much they were earning. The newest guy on the show was prodded to say what he was earning. It was his first regular gig so he was "only" earning $10,000 an episode. The guy who played the stud had been on some other shows so his quote was close to $25,000 an episode. Chris Elliott hated this stupid truth or dare game and only admitted to a ballpark figure in the low thirties per show.

I, of course, was squirming in my seat. I felt invisible. I was like the maid they were talking in front of, who didn't exist. They were talking money—how much they were getting on that show and how much they had earned on other shows and what other opportunities were ahead for them. They didn't think to involve me and that was fine. I excused myself and headed back to my little dressing room. I hated to make any fuss about money, but making about $1,800 for that week, I realized I wasn't really as part of the group as I thought I was.

On all the shows I'd done before, I had never been totally cut. I should have played it safe and waited until after I found out that I had made the show to let my mother know about it.

My mother does not take the normal ups and downs of life very well. If I have nothing going on, she'll usually say, "So, that's it? More disappointments?" It's frustrating knowing that just me being myself without any achievements is letting her down. When my mother calls, a guest spot gives me something to tell her. Then she's like a shark that you feed a sliver of meat to. It's never enough. "Is that it? Anything else coming up? Is that all you have?"

One time, as she kept hammering me, I assumed the part on *Raymond* was safe, so I fed it to her.

After I was cut, she said, "Freddie, why do you think they took you out of the show? Did you do anything to annoy them? You know how sometimes you can be too much. Were you being pushy? Were you being a hypochondriac?"

No matter how much I explained, she couldn't understand that these things just happen sometimes.

Even though my lines were cut, I was still in the background in the wedding ceremony scene, which qualified me for a residual check. Months later, I bumped into Ray on the lot where his show was filmed. I appreciated how he thought to ask if I'd gotten a check and whether I had made my health insurance. I was glad to tell him that I had.

I felt more consolation when my friend, Steve, who was on the writing staff, told me that they still liked what I did, and the main thing was that I had established myself as "the cousin." Now, if any other family gathering would come up on the show, I'd have a good chance of being on that episode.

Two seasons after my first appearance on *Everybody Loves Raymond* I was back. Phil Rosenthal, the creator and showrunner, and Ray Romano joked with me on the set that most likely I'd be cut from that episode too. I knew that was impossible. I was cherishing one of those rare confident moments in show business. The episode was titled "Cousin Gerard" and the whole plot was about my character. It was my largest guest star part. I was in all the scenes but one, so cutting me from that one would be an impossibility.

In the episode, Ray's mother persuades him to give me a job as an assistant for the sports book that he's writing. After my first day of work, Ray comments to his wife, Debra how annoying it is to work with me. He says that I always find something negative to say, even when he compliments me, and that I always complain in that whiny nasally voice. Ray is then taken aback when Debra comments that the two of us share many of the same mannerisms. Later on, Raymond's brother and father reiterate the horror of our similarities, but they also add how annoying I am.

"You think I'm like him. And you think he's annoying. So you think I'm annoying too," Ray says.

Instead of Raymond fixing what he dislikes about himself, he tries to fix those traits in his cousin. He tries to adjust my posture, forces me to smile, and tells me to say the word "now" instead of "neow." I end up storming off and quitting my job after I rattle him when I tell him how annoying he is.

I returned to *Everybody Loves Raymond* over the next five seasons for five much smaller guest roles. And each time I cautiously called the production office to see if I made the cut before informing my mother I was on.

"Is it a big or a small role?" she'd always ask.

"Small," I'd answer as I'd hear more heartache on the other end.

On the episode titled "The Cult," where Ray's brother Robert joins a cult, the whole scene where I enter his apartment and talk him into joining up was cut. Only two other lines of mine ended up remaining. After being informed what to prep my mother for in the length of the decimated part, I found myself temporarily brainwashed by her. I wondered if I was in fact annoying anyone on the set and that was the reason they cut most of my lines. Was I trying too hard to talk about the stand-up days with Ray? Was I asking Peter Boyle too many questions about what it was like working on one of my favorite films *Taxi Driver*? Should I not have asked Doris Roberts if orange juice and bagels and lox are bad for your stomach? Did I piss off Patricia Heaton when I didn't take her up on her offer to marry her live-in nanny so she could become a U.S. citizen?

I was actually quite flattered at first when Patricia wanted to set me up with her Swedish nanny. I went to Ray and asked if he knew anything about the nanny.

"Well, it sounds exotic, a Swedish nanny, but well, I don't want to say more," Ray said.

But then I walked by the prop room and saw that Patricia was asking a group of crew guys if they were interested in marrying her nanny. I felt like such a fool. Here I was thinking she thought I was a desirable, attractive man suitable for her nanny, and she was randomly throwing her proposal out to anyone who would listen.

26

SOME FRIENDS

Around the same time I made my first *Raymond* appearance, I had another big opportunity—a guest spot on the massive hit *Friends*. Needless to say, I was a little nervous before the start of the table reading. If I stayed the week and didn't get cut, I was going to make $35,000! Well, that was according to my fellow actor friend, David. "You'll make $4,000 for the week, and a show like *Friends* will be rerun twice in primetime! And there'll be a few foreign checks, and I bet it'll be in syndication for fifteen years!" But then again, every time I eat out with David, he never factors in tax, tip, or beverages when the check arrives.

I got to the stage early at Warner Brothers Studios, sat at the table, circled all my lines in the script, and muttered them to myself to prepare the best that I could. I had auditioned for the show to play the part of an owner of a restaurant. I didn't get it, but a few episodes later I was brought in to play a waiter where Monica worked as a chef. I was among the annoying staff giving her hell because the chef we liked was fired to make room for her. In the episode, she hires Joey just so she can fire him to look tougher to teach us a lesson.

I looked at my watch and saw I still had fifteen minutes before the others would start milling in. I got up and asked a production assistant where the restroom was. "Follow me," he said as he escorted me around the back of the set and up the stairs while he looked over a slew of keys he removed from his pocket. We walked down the upper level of this narrow hallway and then he stopped at this room. After trying several different keys, he opened it up and indicated for me to go in.

"It's not a bathroom. This is a room," I said

"It's your room for the week. You got a bathroom in it," he said, indicating for me to enter.

I was stunned. I'd never even had a room that was on the same stage I was working on. Most times they had me in a room that was so small and far from the stage, there was no point in even staying in it.

I entered the room, shut the door, and walked around like I had awoken in a dreamy tropical paradise. There was a couch, a phone, and yes, there was a bathroom. I knew Joel was waiting expectantly to hear of the perks on my new show as always. Sorry to disappoint, Joel, but after my week on *Friends*, I'd opt for great comfort over great food for my TV visits every time. Not to get graphic, but I'm not great with public restrooms. I can use them if I have to, but it's easier without crew people, extras, and audience members coming in and out when trying to use it. I realized this was one perk Joel would perhaps not want to live vicariously through me.

When I stepped out of my room to return to the table reading again, the cast and crew had arrived. I saw Matt LeBlanc for the first time that week. It had been over five years since our little tenure together on the forgettable *Vinnie & Bobby*. I was wondering if he was so big now that he didn't want to be bothered with anyone like me from his pre-star days. He happened to be very glad to see me. We talked just a little about our *Vinnie & Bobby* experience.

"Remember how they used to dress you up? They made you look so stupid with that tank top and all those bandages all over your arms," Matt said.

I didn't want to tell him that no one put bandages all over my arms. They just happened to be there. I don't know why, but I always seem to have a cut I don't know how I got, on one of my limbs. I wasn't aware how peculiar bandages were and that they helped accentuate the pathetic cartoon-like character I played on the show.

Turned out my top-of-the-line guest star dressing room was next to David Schwimmer's. To answer the question often asked about the cast, yes, they were friends off-set. I'd pass his room on the way to mine and see all the guys in there on a break playing a PlayStation racing car game. Matt told me that there was no one star of the show. He said if any of them ever got an ego for whatever reason, the others would kick that one in the butt and straighten them out.

I had one of those tricky little off-center parts. I had just a few lines scattered about in two scenes. First I tormented Monica, then she fired Joey and made us all see she was not to be messed with. When I entered the kitchen to give Joey all the Christmas tips he had coming to him, I had to say, "Hey Dragon, here's your tips. And it never hurts to wear tight trousers." After a run-through, Lisa Kudrow (Phoebe) was kind enough to tell me I was doing a good job.

"Those small parts are the hardest to nail," she told me. "I had a recurring role as a waitress on *Mad About You* and having to come on and do just those few lines out of context were harder than what I do now." I was happy to have that issue validated by such a high-level player.

I remember being on the sidelines at a *Seinfeld* taping and watched with horrific empathy as a guest actor flubbed his line. I heard Larry David say, "One line, he's got one line and he messed it up!" That's also what makes it so hard. You're not supposed to mess up one line because it's just one line. How could you?

During the taping, I managed to get the weird words right about how tight trousers get big tips, and I got fairly big laughs. I also scored some more laughs when I locked Monica in the freezer to taunt her some more.

Some writers said it would be great to bring me back, but that there were six characters they had to deal with and it's not that often that they have a story line that involves Monica at her job. But if and when they do . . .

Over three seasons later I was standing around the *Friends* soundstage and watching Jennifer Aniston get out of her car. The security guard approached her, ready to escort her to the table read to start her week of work. She saw me, came over, and gave me a nice hug. (I don't see how you could get a "bad" hug from her.) "Welcome back," she said.

I was very surprised I had returned as the waiter at Monica's restaurant. Returning to a show is like a murder investigation: the longer time passes, the more your hope diminishes.

At the table read I was so excited. Most of the cast knew me from the episode I did years earlier. One of the writers greeted me and said, "I told you we'd work you back in when we had a story that got Monica back in the kitchen."

I told him how grateful I was. I then sat down by the little paper placard with my name written at the table. I was feeling very comfortable since I'd worked with all the producers before and even knew them from their previous shows. I had made four appearances as Fred, a delivery guy, on *Jesse*, a short-lived show starring Christina Applegate. And on their other show *Veronica's Closet* I played the part of a savant on a plane ride. I got to meet Pete Rose who also guested on that episode. It was quite surreal that after a rehearsal, he'd clap his hands, pat me on the back, and say, "Good job! You're doing a good job!" It was as if I were in a fantasy baseball league and I had scored a homer and he was greeting me at the plate.

The table read went fine. No major laughs for me. This other guest actor on the show told me that he thought the story line that we were both in seemed weak. He was nervous that it might be cut out. I agreed, but I felt the writers would rewrite it. It was a strange time for the show. Matthew Perry (Chandler) was in rehab and the producers were not sure if he would make it back to finish the season. They were hoping he would return and tape his segments separately so they could insert them in.

Friends had just a table reading and no rehearsal on Mondays. So after the table read we were dismissed. At about 10:00 PM I got a call from one of the producers that the story line I was in just wasn't happening and that they rewrote it in a different way. My part was written out. He assured me it had nothing to do with my performance at the table read. He said it's not like they were replacing me with another actor. I had seen it happen to others.

I was hoping the cast would ask for my phone number and call me up as a group and say, "Fred, we're bummed your story line got written out. We all think you're great." But I did look at the bright side. Work was work and getting it here and there was still something. And I'd still get paid. I just wouldn't get any residuals. And I did get that hug from Jennifer Aniston.

When my scene was written out of *Friends*, I told myself not to take it personally. My frantic pep talks to myself really sunk in the following season when they brought me back again.

Monica was back in the kitchen. She feels bad that Chandler, her husband, didn't have a bachelor party, so she hires a stripper for his party. In my scene you find out that the woman I recommended was a hooker and not a stripper. I was fairly confident I'd make it to the end of the week. I was a plot point.

We had had the Wednesday run-through and I was feeling good. When it feels like it's clicking, I'm not as anxious to check for the revised script by my door late at night to see if my lines are still in the script or not. I was getting nice smiles, it just felt right. But I happened to wake up as I usually do in the middle of the night and I went for the door. One thing I learned being around crazy show business is you never know. Yes, I was feeling good, but I felt good that other time I was written out at that table read.

"Fred, stop obsessing and find your little part and reassure yourself it's in so you can fall back asleep," I told myself.

I was a little sleepy, a little out of it as I skimmed the pages looking for the character "Fred" I was portraying.

"Ok, don't freak out," I told myself after the first time scanning the script and not seeing my character's name. I looked again and still didn't see it. Not again. Oh well, what can you do? I'll get paid for the week. There are bigger injustices than this I suppose. But then I came to the scene in the kitchen and I realized that for some reason my character's name was changed from Fred to Stu. That was it. The next day I asked someone about it and they said that they realized that my name was not established the first time I was on. I was so relieved to be back. I didn't ask why the name was changed.

I was so excited about returning and staying the week at *Friends* I didn't even care that I didn't get the great dressing room with the phone and bathroom I had the first time. I got a flimsy little room outside the stage that was bare and shook each time someone walked past it. I found out that all the choice rooms for the guests were torn down to make room for a private gym for the stars of the show.

Joel, being the great friend, was utterly incensed they did that to me. He suggested I complain to someone on the show about what they did to our rooms. "Our rooms?" Those guys had the right to do whatever they wanted to fix up their place. That's like if a friend complained that instead of me spending money to buy a new couch for him to sleep on when he stays at my place, I used that money to buy myself a stereo.

27

NORM STOLE MY JACKET

I said to myself, "I've got to stop being so afraid all the time. I've got to change my strategy. Maybe I've been this visiting guy who's always afraid of making waves for too long, and maybe I should be more ballsy."

All of those self-examining thoughts raced through my mind after getting a week's worth of taunting on Norm Macdonald's first self-titled sitcom *Norm*. I was playing a pathologically shy guy and Norm played a social worker. I hoped I could be one of the recurring nuts that come by for counseling.

Norm was a ball-buster who preyed on my vulnerability. I told him how much I liked his impression of Quentin Tarantino on *Saturday Night Live* and he harshly remarked, "That's a great thing to bring up. That was the last show I did on *SNL* before I was fired. That's real nice of you!"

Luckily I realized quickly most of his bullying was for comic relief and after a while, it was sort of fun, I had to admit. True to when I was a kid, I actually preferred a certain degree of taunting to feeling invisible. And maybe I unwittingly helped set up that dynamic. Even though Norm was a pain in the ass, I felt connected to the show. I opened up and told him I had written a movie called *Ski Potty* because I thought I had a contact with a producer of cheesy ski comedies. I never had any pretense about it. I knew it was silly and lowbrow. It was a story about a pathetic guy who buys a port-a-potty, attaches it to a snowmobile, and charges people to use his mobile bathroom at a ski resort.

I'd be standing with a group of people, and Norm would say "Hey, tell everyone about your movie *Ski Potty*."

He never missed an opportunity to embarrass me. "I heard Al Pacino is really interested in this new hot script *Ski Potty*."

If I mentioned a woman I had a date with, or if he saw me talking to a woman on the set, he'd say, "Look at you. You are a sexual predator! Look at Fred!" Other people's suffering seemed to ignite Norm. He'd often pull together a group just to have me repeat stories he liked.

"Tell them what your mother says when she calls you up."

So I'd tell how she asks, "Anything good happening, or the same?"

He'd make me retell the story about humiliating myself with Billy Crystal. Norm played another ball-busting game where he'd purposely misinterpret something you'd say and fake unbelievable shock. For example, I'd say, "I have an audition next week for this other show."

"What!? You're quitting this show midweek to work somewhere else?! That's terrible. That's so unprofessional!"

Still, Norm could be fun. There wasn't pressure about messing up because the set had such a loose feel to it. We'd talk about everything but the show. It was almost an afterthought to him. When I mentioned that I had gotten into tennis lately, Norm joined a court right by the studios. He soon seemed in a rush to get through rehearsals so we could get more time on the court. It was a stuffy place, so they weren't crazy about Norm's playing style, which involved cursing, throwing racquets, and taunting me when he scored a point. When I'd miss a shot, he'd run right up to me, laugh in my face, and raise his fist in the air, screaming, "Yes! Sweet! Yes!"

On Friday's tape night, until just before taping started, I was playing tennis with Norm and Artie Lange, who played Norm's brother. We were getting all sweated up. I asked Norm, "Shouldn't we get back and get ready for the show?" It was obvious he didn't care. It was his show, so I thought, "What the hell." I didn't really have any lines to memorize anyway; because of my character's acute shyness, all I had to do was mumble inaudibly. We made it back to the set with moments to spare.

Hanging out during a break, Norm managed to indirectly taunt me some more. Laurie Metcalf was a regular on his show also. She had co-starred for ten seasons on the hit series *Roseanne.*

"In your ten seasons on *Roseanne*, did any of the guest actors end up becoming famous?" he asked her.

She thought about it a few moments. "No, none that I can think of."

On ten seasons of *Roseanne*, hundreds of guest actors must have passed through, and she could think of none who had hit it big. There, of course, were the special guest stars on *Roseanne*, Martin Mull, Fred Willard, Sandra Bernhard, but that was different. They were already famous.

If Norm had meant to throw me into career despair, he'd done a great job. Were the actors doing these guest star parts stuck in a cycle from which it was impossible to ascend? Was I one of them? I had always figured that all these guest star parts would accumulate and snowball into something big. I thought about it some more and figured I was overreacting. *Roseanne* was just one show. There had to be other shows with dozens of guests who rose higher than that.

My thoughts then turned to an overcompensating "I am going to conquer the world" pep talk. I will be the first multi-year guest star actor who hits it really big. From then on in, others will try to emulate my career. They will push their agents for any delivery-guy parts or any peripheral cousin parts that they could find! And if that doesn't happen, I told myself that there were scores of actors on the same route I was on that ended up having very respectable careers. Okay, not everyone was meant to be a star like Mike Myers or Steve Martin. And then I asked myself, "Why *can't* I be big like Mike Myers or Steve Martin?" Just because they hit it big right away and I didn't shouldn't mean the big dream is over for me. Then I wished Norm had never asked Laurie Metcalf that question in the first place. He knew that would mess me up.

But as with a lot of Norm's comedy, he had struck an uncomfortable truth.

I'm pretty sure taking our tennis matches outside my appearances on Norm's show may have cost me thousands of dollars. After appearing twice as a pathologically shy guy who worked where Norm played a social worker, I was told I was going be a recurring character until I spoke up for myself.

A week after my second appearance, Norm and his assistant showed up at my apartment. He wanted to play some more tennis. I got in his assistant's car and after we played a few hours and Norm defeated me, I forgot my nice new denim jacket in his car. For days after, I asked him to return it, and he'd wave his hand dismissively, "Oh, that jacket. You and that jacket."

Then I made a mistake one night and vented to a date about the jacket. At the end of the night, she got a little upset when I made a pass at her. "All you men with your urges!" she said as she stormed out of my apartment. Since this woman was the only one I told about the incident, I'm certain she was the one who went on Norm's fan site pretending to be me, cursing Norm out, saying he stole my jacket. Norm's right-hand woman found out and called me up asking why I was belittling Norm on his website. I tried explaining I wouldn't do such a thing, and if I did, would I use my real name? It made no sense. The damage was done though. For the next two seasons I didn't return until the very last episode of the series. Eventually I bumped into Norm's assistant who was nice enough to run to Norm's house and bring me back my jacket.

28

MY REAL GOOD DEMO REEL

I stood outside the guard gate at Warner Brothers Studios. A production assistant for the recently canceled *The Brian Benben Show* was doing me a favor. She was coming out to give me a video duplication of the episode I had appeared on. That was my only way of getting a copy of it because the show was axed before all the episodes were aired.

I played Bernie, the ultimate sports collector. I owned a sports bar and some great sports legends were at the opening of my restaurant. Sadly it was the last appearance of Olympic track star Florence Griffith Joyner. Shortly after appearing on the show, she tragically died of an epileptic seizure. Also joining her on the show were two former Los Angeles Laker stars, Kareem Abdul Jabbar and Kurt Rambis. Jabbar had a reputation for being aloof his whole NBA career. After watching him film one of his other scenes from the sidelines, I told him he did a really good job.

"Really? You really think so?" he excitedly asked.

I saw that this seven-foot intimidator was a little insecure and just needed to hear he was doing a good job. Brian Benben who starred in the critically acclaimed HBO show *Dream On* was now playing a news reporter. I felt the show was very strong and was surprised it never got a shot. There was grumbling on the set that CBS wasn't really behind it and they were looking to introduce Ted Danson's new show *Becker* in that spot instead.

I was sorry it didn't air. Obviously Brian Benben must have been more disappointed than I was. I intended to put my scene from the show on my demo reel. I felt it would showcase me in a different light than other clips I had that were edited onto the reel. Benben's character was trying to interview me, but I was so excited, I talked faster than my usual droll, low-key way of talking.

An actor uses a demo reel as a way for casting agents, directors, agents, etc. to get a sense of their work. It's also a way to encompass their total range of work and show their high points. It used to be expensive to go to an editing facility to pay for editing time to construct my demo reel. I'm lucky that my friend had the equipment and was very generous in helping me edit it.

Also on the reel was a clip of me from HBO's *Thirteenth Annual Young Comedian's Special.* Of course I had my *Seinfeld* clips on it. I had a segment of me doing some of my stand-up comedy jokes on the Comedy Central animated show *Dr. Katz, Professional Therapist.* That was a fun, unique show where comedians did their act and were animated as if they were patients talking to Dr. Katz, their therapist. The style of animation was one they invented called Squigglevision, which was basically a drawing shaking back and forth.

After it had aired, a person on the street told me they saw me on the show and liked what they saw. Obviously this person had to know me from something else. No one seeing that show would be able to spot who the actual person was supposed to be based on its crude blurry style, although it still was fun to see myself animated.

The scene from *The Brian Benben Show* was inserted onto the reel and I had twenty new copies made at my favorite video house, and I had someone important to show the tape to.

In Los Angeles, people hardly ever walk the streets. It's just not really done. The town is massively spread out and it's rare that the three things you need to do are within a four-block radius. People think you're a mental patient if you're over thirty-five and walking by yourself in L.A. A woman from one of my former acting classes used to wait tables at a restaurant by my apartment. Once when I was walking by she came out and had to say something.

"Hey, um, I see you walking by all the time. What's wrong?"

But I like to walk. I like to find the places where others might be so I can feel I'm interacting. I'll find a mall. If you're walking around a mall you can pretend you're shopping and seemingly have a purpose. And when I walk, I hope something might happen that will change my life. It's the same hope as when I check my voicemail or e-mail messages. I just hope that getting out of my house will lead to some miraculous chance encounter.

Perhaps that's why I put so much pressure on my demo reel when I bumped into film director Amy Heckerling at the Beverly Connection mall. Her daughter had recognized me from *Seinfeld* and that started a little conversation. Amy Hecklerling was the director of such films as *Fast Times at Ridgemont High*, *Look Who's Talking*, and *Clueless*. She had actually seen me twenty years earlier when I first started out as a comedian in New York City. After our friendly talk, she asked who my agent was. I mentioned them and not to my surprise, she had never heard of them. Then being a bit brave, I asked if I could send her my tape. (I suppose I learned nothing from my harsh initiation to Hollywood when Billy Crystal slammed me for asking if I could send him one.) Apparently I didn't "push it" too far with her and she said to call her office and her assistant would give me her home address for me to send it. I was excited. I thought she'd watch it and maybe have me in mind for something she was working on.

I brought the tape to the post office after anxiously deciding what my cover letter should say. I called a friend and he said the simpler, the better. It was two lines: "It was great bumping into you last week. I hope you enjoy the tape."

I put that note and tape into a padded envelope, but was still a little nervous. Even though I had checked it seven times, I was worried I might have put a porno tape by accident in with a cover letter cursing her out. Of course that was impossible because at the time I didn't own any porno films. I was nervous, but no, I would fight my OCD and not reopen the envelope. I'd be brave and trust my feelings that I checked it well enough.

At the post office, I put the envelope through the bulletproof case enclosure and told them I wanted to send it first class. The postal worker then, to my horror, stamped it "First Class." Well, actually in my scared mind she came down full force on the package smashing it as if she were killing a bug.

I went home and called my friend asking him whether stamping the package breaks the video. He said probably not, but I should have sent it in a cardboard box instead of just a paper envelope. Now I really was nervous.

"But it wasn't just paper. It was lined with that bubble protective stuff."

"It probably will be fine. But I'm just saying that when you ship a video out, it's better to put it in those cardboard boxes because they throw things around from the bin to the truck and you want the best protection."

Now I was picturing her getting the package, opening it up, and either seeing it in little bits or finding out it didn't work. I would feel so stupid. I'd probably never get a second chance to send another tape. My friend said it wasn't a long trip so chances were it wouldn't get tossed around that much in the truck. But I had to hang up and reassure myself.

I took another demo reel I had and put it into another identical envelope and sealed it. Then I smashed down on it pretending I was the postal worker stamping it first class. I even stamped it a little harder. Then I threw it aside on my floor in my imaginary bin and then around my room as if that's what it might have gone through on its tumultuous one-day journey from Los Angeles to Beverly Hills.

I then opened the package, put the CD in my machine, and then the moment of reassurance—it worked! A week later I got a call from Amy Heckerling saying thanks for the tape and that she and her family enjoyed it. To this day, nothing has happened for my career as a result of that, but at least she didn't put something in that didn't work because of a stupid envelope.

29

LOOKING FOR MY TV DHARMA

The producers for the ABC show *Dharma & Greg* were great to work with, but a little bizarre to audition for. Dharma and Greg were a mismatched couple who got married on their first date. Greg was an uptight conservative lawyer and Dharma was a free-spirited new-age yoga instructor.

Dharma had a pirate radio station in her apartment and I was reading for an off-camera role of a nut calling her show. I was ranting that there was a conspiracy in Major League Baseball because of all the home runs being hit all of a sudden.

As the casting woman walked me to the room for my reading, she was courteous enough to warn me that the producers wouldn't be looking at me. She said that they'd be sitting there with their heads down trying to imagine how the lines would sound in context.

I pictured them sitting there with their heads down and politely sticking their arms up so we could shake hands when we were introduced. But they greeted me warmly and then dropped their heads and closed their eyes. I looked at them only briefly sitting there with their heads down, almost like they were in shame. I felt as though I were auditioning for my mother.

I got the part and found myself at another table reading where the staff was all so upbeat. They talked about how they felt that their last two episodes were right back on track to the way they all gelled the first few seasons. I didn't know what that meant, but I clapped along with some others who applauded with enthusiasm. It was infectious seeing how they enjoyed their work and how they felt they were recapturing some of their old magic.

I also might've been applauding a little out of automatic pilot. I decided somewhere along the line that it would be best for me to always appear excited and supportive for whatever show I was on. I thought if someone important should look over at me, I wanted to appear to be a positive factor. Basically I smiled as wide as I could, applauded, and tried my best to do a fake chuckle when everyone else was cracking up, though many times I didn't know why they were.

I never suspected that this fifth season of *Dharma & Greg* would be their last. It all seemed to be going so strong when I joined them at the beginning of that season. But the network was anxious to push an hour-long game show hosted by former tennis star John McEnroe called *The Chair*. For six weeks they were preempted by this show where contestants would sit in a chair that registered their heart pressure.

In fact, in the last few seasons, sitcom opportunities had greatly diminished due to the explosion of game, magazine, reality, and hidden camera shows. In my last two pilot seasons, I had only a fraction of the auditions I had the years before that. Every network wanted the next big unscripted show. They were cost-effective since there are no expenses for union writing staff, actors, or elaborate sets.

I had mixed feelings when the current scary trend of game shows and reality TV began. I had seen and appeared on so many bland and repetitive shows, so I sort of understood the over-saturation of their tired format. Yes, I was concerned. But I was almost used to concern. I never had a mid-life crisis. I didn't need mid-life for it. I was almost always in one. Perhaps those lulls would propel me to some unforeseen path, I had hoped. But I realized I couldn't do what Joel Murray was smart and passionate enough to do. He was directing the episode I was on as well as playing Dharma and Greg's old-time friend, Pete. Directing would not be an option for me. I have no technical or mechanical skills whatsoever. I have to admit I haven't amassed any other possible vocation while observing all the goings-on on all my guest star visits. The only other skill I have is maybe being the guy that answers the stage phone. I have gotten good at talking on the phone on the side without everyone going, "Shush, we're working here!" Yes, I am proud that on all the sets I have been on only a few times have the assistant directors run over to me telling me I am disturbing the show and costing the production and the economy millions of dollars.

Many TV sitcom directors are from shows and films from years past. Like Murray, being a regular on a show, they have the luxury of observing and learning the process. But more important than just the on-the-job schooling, they also have the strong contacts of getting a shot to break in. Many actors actually have it in their contracts to direct a show.

I've crossed paths with Joe Regalbuto from *Murphy Brown* when he was directing an episode of Norm Macdonald's show. I was directed on *Murphy Brown* by Peter Bonerz who I had first seen playing Jerry, the dentist, on *The Bob Newhart Show*. Ted Wass, formerly of *Soap* and *Blossom*, directed the *Jenny* episode I worked on. And former teen heartthrob turned director Robby Benson directed me on *The Naked Truth*.

The producers of *Dharma and Greg* told me at the end of the week that they wanted to bring me back for an on-camera part, and they did. A few shows later there was an episode where Dharma decides to stay true to her free-spirit roots and live in an art exhibit. An old boyfriend of hers sets up a bedroom set in a museum and the two of them live there on exhibit as a performing art piece. I played a guy who tries to pick up women by commenting on the brilliance and significance of the exhibit. That episode was directed by Ted Lange, who played Isaac, the bartender, on *The Love Boat* for a "whole decade," as he referred to it.

I have found that all these actors-turned-directors still love talking about the shows everyone knew them from. On a break, I could ask them any trivial question about their old show and they'd joyfully reminisce about it and then some. None of them ever copped an attitude and said, "Look, I'm a director now. That acting thing is over!" Some former actors-turned-directors still have a little bit of an ego and love to hold court. You can tell it's very important for them to crack up the crew with their jokes and their long-winded theories about life and the business. They still needed some of the attention they used to get.

On tape night for my second *Dharma and Greg* appearance, the studio warm-up announcer introduced Ted Lange as the director of that episode and the crowd gave him a big excited round of applause. You could see Lange beaming as he waved to the crowd. He knew they still loved and remembered him.

But once in a while, I have to bear the brunt of an annoying director who has less power than the show's stars and takes out his frustrations on guests like me. Most sitcom directors I have worked with have been more than pleasant. It just gets a bit wearisome when we guests feel the director is picking on us a little because the big stars of the show might not be taking him so seriously, and the director needs to muscle someone. He'd perhaps keep giving us the same direction over and over, even if we were actually doing what we were being told.

I suppose for the directors to not be a pain, they have to push their egos aside. I could understand how it must be frustrating. On four-camera sitcoms at least, the director doesn't have the same vision and control as the director of a feature-length film. Sitcoms are mostly a writer's medium. Almost always, the one calling the shots is the showrunner—the writer or creator of the show. Sometimes the executive producer at a run-through will give a different way to go than what the director was instructing. It makes it easier when I can approach the director with my dilemma without him caring that he might be undermined. I need to be able to say that yes, he had a certain direction, but the executive producer was telling me something else.

I heard about a conference after a run-through where the producer wanted to fire a guest star actor because he was playing his part way too big. The director wouldn't admit he was the one who told the guest to be so over-the-top. Luckily the star of the show had seen that the guest was only doing what he'd been told and stopped the unnecessary firing.

I once had a guest star booking on a sitcom pilot, which meant my part wasn't considered big enough for the network to pay money to hold me exclusively if the show got picked up by the network. The cast was mostly all unknowns. The director was a good man, but he had a set of rules I had never seen the likes of before or since.

It was at first interesting that every cast member had to sit in a circle and tell a little bit about themselves. Then we got a lesson in stage terminology. We were drilled with "upstage," "downstage," "center stage," and other terms I have hardly ever heard muttered on a set. Usually they just tell you where to stand and then put a little piece of tape where you're supposed to be. Pointing or saying, "Go by that prop over there" has worked fine for ages in television.

But this director thought those terms were so important, we had to stand on the stage and walk in each direction when he called them out in a nerve-wracking final exam. He had a rule that every actor, when they weren't in a scene, had to have their script and a pen in hand in case he had an important note for another actor, so you'd be ready to write that in while you were observing. Every time an actor was late or didn't have a pen or their script with them, he said that penalty was the loss of one of their lines. I don't recall any actor losing a line because of this, nor do I think he had the ability to enforce it if that rule had been broken.

No matter how small your part, you had to do improvisational exercises before the first time you rehearsed your scene. I played a henpecked husband of an overbearing relative. I only had five lines where I was cowering at my demanding wife. Before we rehearsed, we had to improvise the whole chronology of our relationship. We had to "reenact" our first date. We had to act out our honeymoon, followed by our first anniversary, all the way up to the present. I remember standing there so uncomfortably in front of all the crew meandering about on the set watching this.

"Clear the set! Fred is embarrassed!" he commanded.

After everyone cleared the set I had to establish this relationship where all I did was essentially nod my head and say, "Okay, don't be mad at me."

One day we had to come to work three hours early to do a whole array of improvisational exercises. He even brought in Ryan Stiles from *The Drew Carey Show* and *Whose Line Is It Anyway?* to oversee the drills. I'm glad some of the actors actually enjoyed some of the games. I myself didn't get it at all. I knew this director had worked on *Everybody Loves Raymond* a few times and I knew there was no way he'd get that hardened veteran cast on the set a second before they had to be there to partake in any such games or exercises. I could just imagine Peter Boyle being told to pretend he was on a camping trip while the person next to him made buzzing sounds like they were a bee.

But I had a lot of empathy for a newer director the time he had to work on Bob Saget's short-lived sitcom *Raising Dad*, which I was guesting on. During rehearsals the director only could look on passively as Saget not only decided what he was going to do, but also what he and everyone else were going to say. When a star who had the enormous past sitcom success as he had gets another show, usually he gets a lot of power. He'd continually throw out the written lines and come up with his rewrites right there on the spot. I was nervous when, right before our big producers' run-through, he had given me a whole different line to present. Would they think I was so brazen to change their lines? I hoped they knew that he was throwing out random lines when he pleased. When the line bombed, he commented, "I can hear the air-conditioning." As a matter of fact, most of his rewrites bombed. Saget claimed the writers weren't being fair and wouldn't laugh because they resented being undermined.

Saget eventually backed off with the on-the-set revisions. He was in fact a great guy, but seemed to suffer from Attention Deficit Disorder. He couldn't stay still. If someone would enter the set, he'd practically stop the rehearsal and work whoever it was that entered as if he were a talk-show host. If he wasn't trying out material on everyone for his stand-up act, it was because he was exhausted from being up late the night before doing a charity event. He admittedly could not turn any of them down.

Before Friday's tape night, Saget confessed that he was nervous that an annoying friend of his might come to the show and he didn't want such a distraction.

"Yeah, I'm nervous. Yeah I get intimidated," he admitted. "I'm just like you. I'm no different than you."

"Yeah, except for the fact that you're a multimillionaire with twenty years of primetime network series combined and you have three kids, and homes in three different states, and you've always had girlfriends."

He thought about it a moment.

"Okay, not *just* like you," he conceded.

30

I AIN'T NO SCRUB

The difference between my table read at *Dharma & Greg* and the first-year show *Scrubs* was that this one was on the upward curve, and the mood really reflected that. Before the table read got started, the actors were horsing around with each other and they knew they were in a good spot. As usual, the showrunner (creator Bill Lawrence) made some announcements, but it was apparent he wasn't stretching to pull something positive out of a tenuous situation like I had seen on some other shows. On *Raising Dad* they were excited when they moved from 104th to 100th place in the ratings.

Scrubs was a show about a first-year intern, J. D. (Zach Braff), working at a hospital. It had a unique mixture of dark comedy, tragedy, and offbeat fantasy sequences. When I appeared on it in 2001, it was critically acclaimed and soaring in the ratings. Everyone was especially excited when Bill Lawrence said at the table read that NBC announced earlier than it usually does that they were already picked up for the next season. He said that they'll all probably get a basket with lots of great gifts. And they applauded, so I and the other guest star actors applauded too.

They all knew that they could count on the show going at least two more years. NBC was heavily promoting them. They were going to run all of their episodes over a week's course to push it down everyone's throats. There was even talk that the next season it would get the coveted Thursday night spot after *Friends*, and it did.

It was an especially upbeat table reading, but it felt sort of like when I go to my friend's house every year for Thanksgiving. The family makes their thanks for something they got that year: "Let's be thankful we got that inheritance from Uncle Ricky and can now add that extra wing to our house," and everyone nods in agreement. The family is so contented and comfortable with everything and then I have to go back home to my small, rented apartment. I don't mean to complain, but after years of seeing the life the regulars have, I can't help but feel that would be nice.

And I do realize it works both ways. Some of my "friends" think I'm living the life. A friend from my stand-up comedy days who has a lot of money from an inheritance was in town visiting. These other guys from the old days convinced him to not take me out to dinner along with them because they thought I didn't need a free meal as much as they did, since I was always working. I briefly dated this actress whose only roles were in the videos *Buck Naked Tennis* and *Buck Naked Line Dancing*. They are exactly what they sound like. She played tennis and danced, naked. We'd watch them together, and when there were segments where she was being interviewed on the sideline, she'd leap up and down saying, "Look, I'm talking! I'm acting! I'm saying words!" But when I got a little part on *Murphy Brown* she showed her excitement for me by exclaiming and crying, "How come I never get to do anything real like you?"

Whatever insecurity I was feeling seeing yet another cast of regulars bask in the comfort of their homey situation was mitigated by the great feedback I got after the reading for *Scrubs*.

I was playing J. D.'s patient, who opted for an operation instead of taking his advice. The stars of the show told me I was good and a few even knew my old stand-up act. Okay, I used to get booed a bunch back then, but it was an ice breaker. When someone says they've seen me somewhere, sometimes there's that long awkward beat before they say if they liked your act or not. One time a guy on the street passed and said, "Hey, I've seen you. You're a comedian," and he kept walking. I stood there as he passed. I almost felt like catching up and saying, "Well, was it good?" Or "What show did you see? That wasn't me at my best."

Right from the start I knew it was going to be an awesome job. Bill Lawrence told me we would go to rehearse, shoot a few takes, and then if I had any ideas we could mess around with the lines a little. I had never heard anything like that from a showrunner before. Usually the pace of a sitcom doesn't permit actors on the set to contribute their own ways of altering their lines. The writers and producers are rarely present at the rehearsal process. Then at the run-through, the presentation of the show is so fast-paced; a scene is acted out and then it's boom, on to the next scene. With a one-camera show it's shot one scene at a time, with several cameras shooting different angles. That slower, more concentrated pace allows you the time to play around with the material.

There have been a few rare exceptions to this though. If you say something off the cuff at a rehearsal, the star of the show might pass on your suggestion to the producers and they will let you have a shot at it. But it's hard to feel so bold and comfortable to suggest fixes on your own. It helps when the star or a writer you might know on the set sets that up for you.

On one of my appearances on *Everybody Loves Raymond*, Robert was lugging a piano into his mother's living room and I was one of many guests not assisting him when he asked for help. A friend that was a writer on the set said they were playing with different excuses why I couldn't help.

"I can't. I have eczema," I suggested. That line didn't make the cut; actually no one's lines made it in. That joke was axed altogether from the episode. But it was fun to participate that way.

In one of my scenes in *Scrubs*, J. D. is enraged because I didn't trust his judgment about my condition and asked others working at the hospital if I should have surgery or not. The way the scene was written, it ended with the janitor exiting my bathroom, which revealed he was the one I listened to over the rookie intern. But during the taping, we were told to keep going.

"The janitor? Why did you listen to the janitor?" J. D. asked me.

"He seems confident."

"That's it. You're not getting chicken."

"No, I want chicken."

I was very excited that those little ad-libs stayed in the show when it aired. After a few more scenes were filmed, we broke for lunch. I was feeling great.

Lunch was served outside. You walked up to this catering truck and had a nice choice of pasta, potatoes, chicken, or fish. I was toward the back of the line behind crew people and lots of extras who played orderlies, visitors, and patients with various bandages and fake blood all over them. I was waiting on the long line for several minutes when the wardrobe guy walked by after busing his tray of food and told me I should go to the head of the line.

"Principal cast is supposed to go to the head of the line and eat first."

Yeah, I knew I was supposed to go ahead on the line. I did, after all, have a speaking part. And honestly, I didn't want to wait on that long line. I was hungry and I was anxious to call my agent and get feedback about an audition I did the other day. Is Matt Damon going to wait twenty minutes for his lunch from some catering truck? It's not just that, but the principal actors have to eat first so they can get back to makeup for touch ups or wardrobe checks. But was I hungrier than all the extras waiting on line in front of me? I wished an assistant director would just guide me to the front and I could just humbly shrug my shoulders to the disapproving looks of the extras that I passed. "Hey, it's not me. She's the one telling me I have to move to the front of the line." I don't know why that was so difficult for me. I don't know why I even had to think about it. It made me think about where I was in my career. Maybe I had hit upon my problem! I suppose the entertainers that hit it big are the ones that say, "I am going to the top and no one is stopping me!" rather than the ones that say, "I'd like to be in showbiz, but um, I'm not in your way, am I? Sorry. Sorry about that."

Fred, go ahead. Do you want to be more than this nervous guy no one notices? I have a speaking part. Now is my turn to be entitled. I am entitled to go to the head of the line!

Don't be such a nebbish. Would Ray Liotta be so wimpy?

Yeah, I am going to move ahead. Maybe if I move ahead my career will take off. This will be the breakthrough that I have been looking for. This will turn it all around. After I eat my chicken and potatoes, who knows what this decisive action will snowball into. I will have it all!

So I started to make a move, but then worried one of the extras would say "No cutting!" and then I'd just have to explain myself. *Yeah, they'd understand. But why should I contribute to their already humiliating experience? Non-union extras are making sixty bucks a day, union ones about a hundred. They have to wait in that special area and once on set, walk back and forth for hours on end with fake blood all over their face. Why just push ahead of them now and remind them during their lunch break they're at the bottom of the totem pole? Let them enjoy their free lunch. Am I like Andrew Dice Clay's mother? (My mother would complain that his mother always pushed ahead of the others at the bakery in Brooklyn because she thought she was better than everyone else.)*

John C. McGinley, one of the stars of the show, said I could sit at his table. I had been validated by some of the actors and recognized by another! And the day's not over yet and the showrunner already indicated they should bring me back as a patient! This is the time! Why waste all the money I spent reading self-help books? I am not a bad person if I go to the head of the line.

So I did it. As I slowly crept to the front explaining "I have a part in the show. I have a colon condition. That's my part in the show."

"I do too!" an extra said as he pointed to the fake blood by his groin area.

"Yeah, but I talk about mine. I have lines."

And I walked ahead. *You did it Fred! You treated yourself like you deserve things! Now maybe your career and life will take a lead from this action!*

And besides, these extras would all do the same in my situation. But by the time I finally did make my move, I had wasted so much time arguing with myself, I already was near the front and I only went ahead of two extras. *Great debate, Fred.*

After lunch I finished up my scenes. Zach Braff's parents had flown in from New Jersey to watch him on a monitor from another room. Some actors were joking around and cursing and a crew member had to tell everyone not to swear because his parents were watching. The parents said that was no problem at all. You could tell they loved watching their son, they were practically lip-syncing along with him. *Oh, so this was what parental pride must look like.*

It's nice working with regular cast stars when they acknowledge how lucky they are. The expression I thought of was the one from *Murphy Brown* said by Charles Kimbrough who played anchor Jim Dial; that it was like he had won the lottery. He had been around awhile doing theater in New York and then got ten years on that show. And then I heard that expression again from a neighbor I always bumped into who got to be a part of the last three years of *Sabrina, the Teenage Witch*. He was very grateful for those three years. And you had to be happy for him. He was always nice and never had any attitude or ego about himself. It was the second time I heard that expression so it was starting to click. The lottery, they won the lottery.

And on the set, Zach Braff also said he felt like he had won the lottery. He was young and he knew he had a great thing going on. He was on a show that was going to have a nice run, and where everyone was having fun and he was making very nice money.

When I was leaving and saying goodbye to him and his other fellow lottery winners, it occurred to me—I worked with fun, receptive people. I was paid a week's worth of work just for the one day, I ate that nice free meal and the producer said that maybe I might come back. But even if I didn't, if only for today, I won the lottery too.

31

THE KING RULES

Caroline Rhea was a bit less than welcoming to me when I returned to *Sabrina, the Teenage Witch*. I got big laughs, and I was excited after doing the table read until everyone got up from the table, and she shook her head in disbelief.

"What? What's wrong?" I asked.

"It makes no sense you're back."

"What do you mean?"

"You were The Butler the first time, now you're The Warning Man?! How could that be?"

"Make sense?" I asked. "This is a show with a talking cat and it's all in the Third Realm, a magical place."

"The *Other* Realm!" she corrected as she stormed away. She headed out and I was nervous. Was she going to tell the producers the mistake they made having me back? I wonder if she had something to do with the fact that there was no third visit.

But I did get invited to the 100th episode party. It was at this new club in Hollywood, seeing everyone who had anything to do with the past 100 episodes. As I passed the casting director, he looked at me and said, "Gee, it looks like they invited *everybody* to this." I just nodded and walked on.

It could've been worse. He could've said, "They even invited idiots who don't know what the Other Realm is!"

Another 100th episode party brought me to the brink when this woman stole my *The King of Queens* jacket. Seeing a pattern with me and jackets?

All I'd done on *The King of Queens* was an off-camera voice-over part. I hardly knew Kevin James, but he set it up so I wouldn't have to go through the ordeal again of having to read in front of the close-eyed producers. I had an audition scheduled for *The King of Queens* when I bumped into him at *Everybody Loves Raymond*'s 100th episode party. I mentioned I was auditioning for his show and he said he'd put in a word. He did and they called and said the part was mine because Kevin said it should be. I have been in many situations where stars I've come across say they're going to do something and they don't. I don't hold grudges. I understand they have a lot on their minds, so when someone comes through like Kevin did, it's a rare unexpected surprise.

It was a fun scene. Kevin was driving his crappy car to a fast food drive-through. I played the voice of the guy taking his order, talking through a plastic clown and then I ask him to please move his car forward. But the car breaks down. Kevin goes crazy when I keep saying, "Please move the car forward," so he takes a bat and pummels the taunting plastic clown.

When I showed up to record the scene, I got *The King of Queens* mug and a nice card from Kevin thanking me for working on the show. It was also signed by his costar, Leah Remini. It's never happened that I have gotten a gift the week I am working. The gifts are usually given out at the wrap, Christmas, or show's anniversary parties. I went to Kevin and told him how much I appreciated it and he told me how much he appreciated me being on his show.

Then around the holidays I got a big box. I was a bit puzzled as I opened it and saw a top-of-the-line leather baseball jacket with *The King of Queens* stitched on the back. And there was a note from Kevin and the other producers wishing me a happy holiday.

I hadn't even been invited to their Christmas party. Usually those big presents are for regular cast and crew or for those that are at least recurring members of the show. I actually bumped into Kevin James soon after at a movie theater and thanked him. He said he loved how the episode came out and really appreciated that I was on his show. This was personal. It was a lot more than a hat you get when you leave a party.

Then I made a mistake. I was on a first date with an actress new to L.A. She was wide-eyed and ready to make it big. We met by the tennis courts near my house. We played and then it got chilly, so I ran up to my place, looked for something to lend her, and spied my new jacket. Hey, this might impress her as well as keep her warm, I thought.

We had dinner at my favorite Chinese restaurant. She seemed a bit disappointed when I told her I wasn't really a celebrity.

"But you were on *Raymond*. I saw you on that show."

Actually, sitting with her, I in fact did feel what it must be like to be a celebrity: she was only connecting to the part of me that had been on TV, not to me at all.

I walked her to her car and I knew she wasn't really into me, but I was in denial. I still was hopeful we'd see each other again. I wanted to seem cool and calm, so I said, "It's cold, hold onto the jacket. Why should you have to drive home being chilly?"

The next day I called and she didn't call back. Finally we talked and she said she was leaving town. Then she mentioned she had a boyfriend. I mentioned my jacket and she said, "Yeah, it looks good. I like it. Yeah, I'll get it back to you when I get back in town."

I wish I was more spontaneous. I hung up and it took a while for me to realize I should have demanded the jacket back right that second. I called but got no answer. I waited a few days and I called again and got no response. I was freaking out.

I had lost jackets to women before. I don't understand that pattern of mine. I had lost a baseball jacket to a woman back in New York. Again, we didn't even date. She tried it on, thought it looked cute on her, and asked to borrow it. Again, wanting to seem like the guy who is cool and uncaring, I said sure. Then I could not reach her. I had lost a leather jacket to a woman who I dated. I could get that back, but once the relationship got weird, I didn't want to call.

I didn't know exactly where she lived. I only knew the block, but I was going to get that jacket back. If I had to, I would walk up and down her block until I found her. I would hang out at The Groundlings, the improvisational theatre I knew she studied at. I would get that jacket back! There was no doubt about it.

Not only did I love it, but the gesture from the cast meant more to me than anything else. It couldn't have been a more personal gift even if Kevin James had delivered it to my place himself. Just as he had made a point to tell the producers to let me have the part, I'm sure he also made a point to include me as one of the special guests to receive the jacket.

It turned out I was paranoid. She was away and finally did call back later that night when she returned. I didn't have to do all those crazy balls-to-the-walls antics to get it back. But I would have.

I am now obsessively careful with my cast and crew leather jackets, especially my *King of Queens* one. When I see an attractive woman wearing an oversized leather film or TV show baseball jacket, I wonder what poor lonely shnook got taken for it.

32

THE QUENTIN TARANTINO DELUSION

Every character actor, me included, has the Quentin Tarantino fantasy. We hope that something iconic we appeared in has stuck with him, and he's been dying to think of a way to use us in some different inventive way in one of his cool, gritty films. Of course this started with John Travolta after he played Vinnie Barbarino in *Welcome Back, Kotter*. He was in the slow part of his career when Tarantino revived him and starred him as a lovable hit man in *Pulp Fiction*. (I've never met a hit man face-to-face, at least that I know of. I'm curious if they're all so charming and love spouting off about pop culture.) Many of us fail to acknowledge in our delusions that Travolta already was quite a star, when he was "revived," but maybe there are reasons we have this fantasy. Besides Travolta, Tarantino also sought out the late David Carradine from *Kung Fu*, and Michael Parks from *Then Came Bronson*, for *Kill Bill* and gave them a big boost.

But my favorite story of a Tarantino revival was of Robert Forster. Forster had a bit of a career for awhile in the '60s and '70s as a tough guy hunk in such films as *Alligator*, *Medium Cool*, *The Black Hole*, and *Avalanche*. And then, like many a career, his plummeted. He'd get bit parts in films, but then told me he went for over 300 auditions without booking a role, so he stopped auditioning. He figured if someone wanted him, they'd give him a part.

Part of his routine was having breakfast every morning at The Silver Spoon on Santa Monica Boulevard in West Hollywood. Before he became a success, Tarantino came into the diner, recognized Forster, and proclaimed he was going to put him in one of his films some day. Though Tarantino's passion for Forster was unmatched, it still had to be the right film. Forster came close to getting a role in *Reservoir Dogs*, and then years later Tarantino came back into the diner and gave Forster a copy of his script for *Jackie Brown*. A few days later, Tarantino asked what he thought of it. Forster said he loved the story, but didn't see any parts he could play. "I was thinking you could be the bail bondsman," Quentin offered.

"No way they're gonna let me play a major role in a studio film," Forster replied. (Pam Grier, who played Jackie Brown, also thought there was no way a studio would let her star in a major film.)

"They'll do whatever I say they should do," Tarantino said. Forster excelled in the part and ended up getting nominated that year for Best Supporting Actor at the Academy Awards. He never thought it would happen, but Tarantino had resuscitated his career

"I got them in the late innings," he'd say.

Before I fell in love with Forster's story, I fell in love with *Jackie Brown* maybe for the same reason. It starred two middle-aged people in a love story. That was so rare. I loved Forster's portrayal of a macho yet sensitive, burnt-out bail bondsman. But what I love most about Tarantino are his interviews, or any chance I get to hear him talk about what he loves to do. I love what he said about *Reservoir Dogs*: "People said they'll never let you do that. Who are 'they'? If you say a 'they' you create a 'they'."

I have coffee every morning at Hollywood's Farmers' Market with a table of older character actors and directors, which includes acclaimed director Paul Mazursky. He's known for some seminal movies like *Blume in Love*, *Next Stop, Greenwich Village*, *Harry and Tonto*, *Down and Out in Beverly Hills*, and *Bob & Carol & Ted & Alice*.

The guys at the table banter, tell bad jokes, commiserate about their medical aliments, and talk about the old days. One day Mazursky announced that Quentin Tarantino was going to make a visit to our morning table. It turned out Tarantino was a big fan of his. I had a gig on *Wizards of Waverly Place* the day he was going to stop by, and I was so excited that the table read was scheduled for later in the day and I'd have the chance to meet him. He was probably the one living person I was most excited to meet. And part of that excitement was the hope I had that being a TV and movie junkie, he would know and love me from *Dumb and Dumber* or *Seinfeld*, or maybe from some crazy obscure little thing. Just him knowing who I was would be so thrilling. But of course, there'd be that other dream that I'd get to play a hit man, or a cop, or Steve Buscemi's brother.

I approached the table, and there he was! I sat down while he was in mid-conversation talking about *Inglourious Basterds*. No one introduced me. The guys asked him questions about how he found the "Jew hunter" for the film. I butted in and asked if Colonel Landa let Shosanna escape and knew he was sitting next to her drinking milk later on. "No, no," he said, pointing his finger. "I don't give away movie secrets." The guys asked more questions about the film. Tarantino told veteran actor George Segal that if *Inglourious Basterds* had been made when he was younger, he would've cast him as the "bear Jew."

I was thrilled to be hearing him talk so passionately about his films and explain things he had probably explained a thousand times in interviews. But he still didn't acknowledge me whatsoever!

He knew Ronnie Schell, an eighty-year-old character actor from *The Strongest Man in the World*, a cheesy Disney TV movie. He knew Jack Riley from *The Bob Newhart Show* and *Spaceballs*. But me, no clue! I told him how much I loved his quote that "if you say there's a 'they,' you create a 'they'."

When it was time for me to go, I said I was working on *Wizards of Waverly Place*. He told me to say hi to "they." I headed off and hoped for the thing every journeyman actor hopes for: that the next Quentin Tarantino, who hasn't made it big yet, will keep me in mind when he casts his movies.

33

TWEEN STAR

I was off to the side on the set of *Wizards of Waverly Place*. I was playing a doorman of the apartment building Selena Gomez's character lived in. My character was supposed to break up a noisy party of zombies, wizards, vampires, and an ogre. My line was "No loud parties, and not only that, you didn't invite me, and I happen to be the life of the party!" And then I had to do a demented little dance showing how "wild" I was.

Selena was teaching me how to do the Dougie, the popular dance. I cupped my hand under my chin, and then swayed and contorted my lanky middle-aged body to the side as I said, "Lean and brush. Lean and brush." I felt like Gumby with the wires removed from it. Selena laughed. Of course I wasn't supposed to be good. I was just supposed to do a moronic version of it.

After scores of traditional, multi-camera sitcoms of the nineties seemed to have vanished, my guest star life revived with the emergence of Disney and Nickelodeon cable series. Though dying on network television, multi-camera sitcoms were huge with teenagers and preteens. I ended up deriving more joy than ever from being the guest star guy for kids. All the parts for adults usually were buffoonish and cartooney. But that was fine because I felt the kids appreciated me ten times more than even the most diehard *Seinfeld* and *Friends* fans did.

From just one appearance on *Drake & Josh* playing Foam Finger Guy, I achieved rock star status with kids, I still have to this day. I loved working on these kid shows because for the most part, they didn't have that self-important pretense network adult sitcoms had. Sometimes, however, the material may have been a bit too over-the-top silly, and not the most sophisticated, like on *Cory in the House* when I was involved in a foodfight and had to slip on a custard pie, or on *Ned's Declassified School Survival Guide* when a kid had gas and we had to duck from the smell. They were all fun, stress-free times, except for two situations on *Hannah Montana* that nearly caused me to have a nervous breakdown.

The first time my agent called saying they wanted me to audition for *Hannah Montana*, it was early in the show's course, and it was not the hit it soon became, or perhaps I wasn't as aware of its strength when well-meaning friends insisted I had to audition for it. I looked it up on IMDb and saw it was run by my old boss, Steven Peterman, who I worked for years earlier on *Murphy Brown* and *Suddenly Susan*. They wanted me to read for the role of a man wearing a silly moose costume complete with antlers, and do corny moose puns ("Moose Springsteen, I love Moosey.")

At that stage in my career, I couldn't bring myself to be the middle-aged guy walking around the set in my moose costume while the bratty stars of the show pushed me out of the makeup chair because they had important things to do. Simply put, I didn't want to do it. I knew too well that if I just came out and said to the producers, "No offense, but playing a moose wasn't something I wanted to do," they wouldn't understand. They'd be offended. Okay, if it were in a Coen brothers movie, yes, I'd gladly put on the antlers.

Every writer and producer thinks their stuff is phenomenal and would take it a little personally if I passed. Since I didn't want to burn a bridge with these producers, I lied. I said I desperately wanted to read for that fun part, but I was doing some animation voiceover work. Being brazen enough to say you don't want to do it never works and only causes you more headaches.

"When are you doing it?" they persisted. "We'll work around your schedule!"

So I had to lie some more. Not only was I having all these "appointments" all over town, being the in-demand Hollywood guy that I was, but I went back to stand-up comedy. I said I was headlining on the road. And that still didn't stop their persistence. "What are your dates? Maybe you can fly back and we'll squeeze the scene in on one day!" Then one of the writers somehow got my phone number and asked what was going on. I told him I was about to leave the country where I'd be telling my jokes in Canada for an indefinite amount of time.

Paranoid about getting caught, I hibernated in my apartment for two weeks. It was getting costly having take-out food delivered, so I finally thought it might be safe to sneak out and get a bite in the outside world. I headed to my favorite spot where I thought I recognized the writer who'd called me. I immediately ducked and hid in a bathroom stall for a half hour.

A few seasons later I was brought to *Hannah Montana* for a part without having to audition. There'd be no idiotic antlers on my head or moose cries. I'd be playing an un-dynamic casting agent. Billy Ray Cyrus was thrilled to be working with me. He was more than complimentary and I appreciated that. Being a teen show, everything was over the top, sort of like vaudeville, but ironically, as I delivered my lines in my characteristic low-key, deadpan way, the producers kept saying I had to bring it down even more. What I ended up doing that made them pleased seemed like Ben Stein on Quaaludes.

After the taping, while I was walking toward my parking spot, Billy happened to stop by in his truck, thanked me again, and said, "We should do a movie together. We're a funny combination." He tipped his hat and headed off.

Nice thing for him to say, but those words almost destroyed me for three weeks. I went back and forth as if this was an opportunity from Spielberg I just had to exploit. Yes, that *would* be a funny combination. He's this burly country Western guy with the big hair and hat, and I'm the skinny neurotic Jewish comic guy. That would be a great movie, right?! Okay, but what would the movie be? And was he serious? I didn't know, but being diligent, I knew I had to follow up with this opportunity. So I went to a video store on Sunset and bought every comedy duo box set I could: Martin and Lewis, yes, that's what we'd be like! I bought *Tenacious D in The Pick of Destiny*, *Cheech & Chong*, and also country and Western albums I wasn't familiar with to be versed in that. I studied the films and albums for days on end.

I agonized what the film should be, and was he really big enough of a star to say, "Hey, this is Fred Stoller and we're gonna do a buddy movie together"? And how would I track him down? I went back and forth, should I write it? Write what? Over and over until the anxieties exploded in my head. Finally, sensibility got the better of me and I realized he was a good guy, but not one who could get a movie done, especially with me playing his sidekick as his selling point.

34

A HANDY GIG

Dan Yaccarino, a successful children's book author, got the green light to cast his Nickelodeon show *Oswald* about a lovable helpful octopus. He deliberately set out to cast it with some of his favorite television character actors. He didn't want to go the typical route of cartooney, over-the-top voice actors. He brought in Michael McKean and David L. Lander (Lenny and Squiggly from *Laverne & Shirley*), Laraine Newman, Fred Savage, Eddie Deezen, Richard Kind, and me. He'd seen me in *Murphy Brown* and cast me as a talking dopey tree for several episodes. We had a lot of fun. Dan told me how much he loved what I did, and again I heard those words, that not *maybe*, but *definitely* he'd have me back for the next season. Unfortunately, there wasn't another season, but almost ten years later when an executive from Nickelodeon moved to Disney and helped create a new show, she remembered me from *Oswald*, brought me in to audition, and really pushed for me for the role of a nervous monkey wrench in *Handy Manny*, an animated show about a handyman and his group of talking tools.

Handy Manny came just when I needed it. I had just come from an audition where I waited an hour to read for a small guest part in a new pilot playing a bellhop. After reading my three lines the casting director said, "Very good, but could you do that without your New York accent? This takes place in San Francisco after all." I said, "Sure, um, no problem." What I wish I said was, "Oh, I forgot. They made that new law that if you move from Brooklyn to San Francisco, you can't get a job at a hotel." Actually what I really should've said, and I do now, is, "This is how I talk. When I try to lose my accent, it doesn't sound natural." So I thought by annunciating each word very deliberately, I could lose the accent. I ended up sounding like someone trying to talk slowly and precisely to a deaf person.

On my way home, my agent called saying my other audition for a casting agent was canceled, but moments later I got a call from my voice-over agent. "You're gonna be on *Handy Manny*! The show got picked up for fifty-two eleven-minute episodes and you're gonna be in every one of them!"

It turned out for almost 200 episodes I had a reprieve from the hustle and uncertainty of scrambling for my next sitcom or movie role.

When I got a taste of the animation world, complaining was impossible. There were no wardrobe fittings, no waiting around all day for a run-through or a tape night, no makeup, or even the need to shave or shower if you were late. And you weren't trembling that your lines wouldn't hit at the taping. They'd make sure they got what they wanted usually in three takes. Each recording was intimate, concentrated on you, and never frantic.

Always a collector of quirky toys and kitschy TV memorabilia, I achieved my dream when a talking action figure was made for Rusty, the nervous monkey wrench I was voicing. Actually, there were dozens of other toys I'd scoop up at the studio, soon making my apartment more like *The 40-Year-Old Virgin*'s pathetic bachelor pad than it already was. But nothing thrilled me like having a talking figure with my own voice! The only problem was that for some reason this action figure was a limited edition, only available in Canada. After losing a fierce bidding war on eBay for it, I convinced a friend, who was working in Vancouver, to buy it for me. But when he brought the toy home and showed it to his two-year-old son, the kid fell in love with it and didn't want to let it go. I had to jump through hoops and buy something else the little boy liked to replace it.

I sent a talking Rusty to my mother who only was concerned with how much money I got for it. She is insanely gullible, and I admit I might've been a bit cruel when I said I got five cents every time the button was pressed and it spoke. But then I felt especially guilty when she called a few days later asking if I got the money because she was pressing it all day.

Going to recording sessions reminded me of when I was a kid and my father would come home from work and I'd run down the steps hoping he'd have a surprise toy for me because of that one time, that did happen. Sometimes there'd be *Handy Manny* blankets, a sweater, knick-knacks, and other fun toys lying around to take.

I got to work with greats like Fred Willard, Jane Lynch, Michael York, Marion Ross from *Happy Days*, and dozens of other loose, grateful celebrities making a cameo. It was in-and-out, easy, fun work. I loved my regular job on *Handy Manny*, but even there sometimes I felt like the outsider. The cast was comprised of animation all-stars who had about a dozen other *Handy Manny* gigs going at the same time. In animation, you knock out your work so much quicker than live action, you can run to another gig, perhaps even several a day—that is if you're "in." There are about twenty-five voice-over actors who do 90 percent of the work. Being "in" means having more range than I do. You can have a unique voice and get lucky, but to do as many as the millionaire all-stars do, your voice can't be that recognizable and you have to alter it to whatever the show needs. And it helps your possibilities of being around if you can do several different characters. They only have to pay each voice-over actor for three separate characters per episode.

At first, I was a little left out of the conversations at *Handy Manny*. The others knew each other very well, having spent years hanging out, doing hundreds of gigs together. The women usually sat together and looked through magazines, waiting for their cues. They were very adept at doing anything that had nothing to do with the show until it was their line; they'd text, read, or gab about expensive home renovations or buying their next home. And then, with a radar sense, they knew it was their turn, put their magazine aside, said something like, "We can fix it, Manny," and then resumed drooling over a photo of an amazing guest house they just had to have.

Sometimes though, their radar sense would be off. An actress played the part of a flashlight who only spoke Spanish. Most of her lines were, "Yupi! Yupi!" I think that meant, "Yippie!" When she'd be reading or texting and it was her line we were waiting for, the actress next to her would elbow her, indicating it was her turn. She never could find her place and always took a shot and said "Yupi!" Half the time her guess was correct.

One time the ladies literally spent thirty minutes talking about a dream bathroom she was hoping to build. One of the guys butted in and suggested a company that only charged twenty grand for bathroom renovations. The women scoffed at him for chiming in with his useless information. They continued talking about the perfect bathroom and one actually said, "Yes, you need luxury, but also functionality is important too." My jaw dropped. Really? Expensive bathrooms also have to function?

It was the easiest job in the world. Most of my lines were, "Oh, no, Manny, I'm scared!", "Do we have to go so high up, Manny!?" or, "I'll stay here where it's safe."

I'd usually have six, or sometimes just three, lines scattered throughout the script. I'd sit, and when it was my turn, stand up, scream that I was scared, and then sit back down.

Handy Manny let me save my money and not have to do things that made me miserable. It helped cut down the showbiz desperation, and I didn't feel I had to constantly leap midway off the toilet for any audition. I started turning down auditions I knew I was wasting my time on, that I had no shot at. And with much of the desperation gone, I was able to try to think how to be more creative as opposed to fruitlessly ramming myself into other people's puzzles so much.

35

BUILDING MY OWN HOME

I was pleading with Sarah Silverman to do a sex tape with me.

"Sarah, I mean you're not doing as well as you used to and if we had a sex tape . . ."

". . . If we had a what!?"

"It's not such a big deal," I said. "Everyone has one. We both could use the Internet buzz. Look, I'll do all the nudity. All the nudity will be on me. I'll cover you."

It was an idea for a comedy segment. After years of being a guest in other people's homes, I decided to somehow build my own. I had an idea for a quirky talk show where I play a delusional security guard on a studio lot who thinks he's a talk show host. Like any other host, I do a little opening monologue, have a sidekick, and do desk and video remote pieces, but all while inside my enclosed booth.

I had this idea for ages but didn't know what to do with it until the web started putting out millions of shorts from comics and everyone else on the planet. It was competitive, but if you had just some money and knew people who knew how to shoot and edit, you could slop together your own segments.

After looking to no avail for a parking lot that had a booth I could shoot this in, I fronted my own money and had these two guys build an actual guard booth. I rented a U-Haul and transported it to a parking lot in the hopes that this web series would go viral and lead to an actual show. I then began the arduous task of convincing celebrities I was acquainted with to drive through my gate/show.

I managed to persuade Sarah Silverman, Bob Saget, Howie Mandel, and Fred Willard to "guest star." We'd shoot them sitting in a car and then use a double to make it look like they pulled up to the gate.

Saget came to the parking lot psyched to help out, but then didn't want people to know what car he drove. Okay, that would be understandable if there was anything that distinctive about his car. So we said we'd supply a car for him, but he didn't like the choice of cars our ragtag group of young camera guys had. I was trying to convince him to just sit in a car, not a horrible one, pull up, and it would all be okay.

"No one's gonna see this," I told him even though I hoped a million people would see it. "The shot of the car will be just a second." He was hemming and hawing. I was scared we were going to lose him. But he finally relented. He said he was going to make a comment that it wasn't his car. He was driving his cousin's. Fine, say anything, as long as we had Bob Saget drive through. And he was great. Our bit was my sidekick and I decide we should give cool gift bags to the guests so they'll tell their other celebrity friends they should be on the show.

Saget drives on and I announce to the "crowd" in my head, "Ladies and gentlemen, Bob Saget! Since I'm hosting a show and you've hosted shows, any advice for me?"

"Show? What show?" Saget responds. "I just want to get on the lot. There's no show here. This is just a security booth."

"Okay, Bob has to go. Let's give him his cool gift bag so he'll tell his other celebrity friends!"

I hand him his gift and Bob looks at the stained bag. "This has obviously been used many times before by other people."

"It's your swag bag for being on our show!"

Saget looks through the bag holding up a used tube of toothpaste, an old cat toy, and some thread. "This is crap. Seriously, you have a job, get one. Open the gate!"

With Sarah Silverman, she would have to sit in a car right outside her house. And I'd learned from the Saget experience.

'We'll get you a nice car," I e-mailed her.

"No, I want to use my car, a shitty car."

I was so relieved she had a good sense of humor and wouldn't be uptight about her image. My bit for her was that when she drove by, I try to persuade her to do a sex tape with me, that it would go viral and we both needed it for our sagging careers.

I usually waited until the last minute to e-mail the script, or just told them what they had to do on the set. It was either because I was tinkering with it till the last second, or I didn't want them to get fixated on any one word and back off. I felt everything could be smoothed out once we were out there. So I sent Sarah the script the morning we were supposed to go out there. I then got an e-mail back.

"Bummer."

I freaked out. Not only did I obviously need a celebrity of her caliber, but I was so pleased she agreed to do it, the last thing I wanted to do was upset her. Part of my character's pitch to do the sex tape with her was that things weren't going so well for her: I say things like her show's been canceled, she hasn't done any movies since *School of Rock*, and Jimmy Kimmel, her ex, is doing so much better than she is.

"Just cause I drive a shitty car shouldn't mean I'm not doing well" was her next e-mail. I freaked out. I e-mailed back apologizing profusely. I never meant to offend her. She also didn't like one of her lines with the word "pussycat."

"Of course! Say anything you want."

My camera guy wasn't sure if he should bother going to her place. Was the shoot off? Finally after a half hour, she got back to me and said it was all cool. I was shaking when I saw her. Now I was back to being the guy on eggshells. We shot the scene in three minutes, and then for the next half hour we had fun telling stories about degenerate comics we knew.

My next little problem was shooting Howie Mandel in just three minutes downtime during a break while he was doing his new series *Mobbed*. He'd be rushed over to sit in my car, and then would have to run back to his show. But I knew Mandel was an admitted germaphobe, so before the shoot I rushed to a car wash, and then had to send it through an additional time just to make sure there'd be no problem.

Mandel did a fun bit where he told a juicy story about seeing one of the *Deal or No Deal* women's naked breasts, but my character is frustrated because the story was drowned out by a gardener using his leaf-blower a few feet away.

And Fred Willard was hysterical playing a clueless celebrity who is brought to our greenroom, which was a tent a few feet away with a nerdy lapdancer.

I managed to sell the show to a website, then had the additional headache of getting the celebrities later on to sign their releases for consent to air on the Internet. Bob Saget signed at first, but then his high-priced lawyer got him very nervous. And though Sarah Silverman couldn't be nicer and more accessible, I was nervous about bothering her again, so I first donated money to her favorite charity for goodwill, e-mailed her the confirmation for the contribution, and then asked her.

I was so thrilled about the possibilities of the show, especially when a friend saw a rough cut of the segments and said they had the fun feel of *Pee-wee's Playhouse*. I thought this was going to take off on the web, and then I'd have my own real TV show!

They aired, and many people seemed to like them and thought it was a great idea, but my illusion of these segments "blowing up" on the Internet didn't exactly occur. But since the feedback was so positive, I wanted to hang onto that guard booth for when at some point I did more episodes. I looked into storage spaces, but because of the size and width of the booth, the cheapest I could find was about $170 a month on the outskirts of town. So I did what everyone does: I asked on my Facebook wall if anyone had a garage or backyard where I could store the booth as a favor.

"I love and believe in your *Gate Show*! I have a big garage I don't use!" a peripheral friend generously offered. So Aaron, my director and builder of the booth, rented a truck and drove the booth to her garage. We slid it on its side, and then she said, "So, how much you gonna pay me?"

"Huh? I thought this was a favor, a belief in my artistic endeavor."

"You said it was gonna cost you at least $170, and I'm a single mom out of work, so what will you give me?"

We were stuck. I offered a price that was too low, so we agreed to $100 a month. Each month when the rent is due, I pay in cash and I meet her at a restaurant that's attached to a video arcade so her kids come along. I end up paying for everyone's meal, and some games for her boys to play. It usually ends up costing more than if I went to the $170 storage space in the first place.

I've made a list of other show ideas, additional celebrities I could pester for more *Gate Show* segments, and if that doesn't work out, I've thought of celebrities I could do an actual sex tape with if all else fails.

36

LIFE IMITATING ART

I had graduated from the annoying pharmacist on *The Nanny* to the annoying waiter on Fran's Drescher's new show, *Happily Divorced*. Fran's character sits down for her first meal at a restaurant all by herself and I make the experience a dreadful one. I humiliate her by screaming out, "She's all alone!" as the busboy empties her table of the extra silverware, and I continually remind her she's all alone when she requests certain specials only available for two or more.

It was sort of ironic that I played this character because the truth is, almost all my meals out, I'm the guy who feels the anxiety of eating alone. You may ask: *How can that be? You're a guy who's been on TV a bunch. You really eat out alone a lot?* Or, by now, you're probably not saying that.

I don't work in an office where there are ladies in low-cut dresses begging to set me up with their friends, or guys who point at their computer screens, showing me the latest video of a cat with Tourette's. I don't work anywhere most of the time, so when I get hungry, I like to get out of my apartment. But I also have found it could be a harrowing experience eating by myself at the wrong establishment.

I wish I could be one of those people who can sit at a restaurant, alone, reading the paper while chatting up the waitress. "So, what's new in your world, Doris?" But I have the social skills of a skittish cat. I know Doris works hard, but . . .

I usually like a place that doesn't have waitress service. I like the freedom to be able to bolt at any moment, so that's why I like paying for my food before I eat. Just last week, I needed to flee desperately. An attractive, annoying couple was sitting in the booth next to me. They did that thing where they didn't sit across from each other, but sat side by side. I suppose they sat like that because they couldn't stand the idea of not having the sides of their hips touching for thirty minutes. Then they started kissing. The only thing more sickening would've been if they took out a wad of cash and started counting and kissing that too.

At another table some idiot started talking very loudly on his cell phone while his baby cried; and he ignored the kid. I gave the kid the stink eye, knowing it would do no good. Only thing worse here would've been if the kid was crying while on a cell phone. Well, maybe not. All I wanted was my check, but of course the waiter was nowhere in sight.

Eating alone is not the worst way to dine. I'd much rather eat alone than eat out with my mother. When I visit her in Florida, I try to avoid TooJays, a Jewish deli in Boca, after we had an incident there. At first I was okay with her continually using her catchphrase (which I've heard my whole life), "It's almost over." She also kept putting her head down, covering her eyes because she couldn't bear looking at the black busboy working there. "I can't look. Black lives are so sad. This is all they have, or prison." I was even patient when she pointed to others from her retirement community and informed me which ones had parts of their bowels cut out. She'd intersperse this with stories of those who'd had strokes and laid on their hot kitchen floor for days until someone found them. I simply nodded, but then, when I got up to use the bathroom, she yelled so everyone could hear, "Freddie, you need to see a doctor. You urinate so much! Why do you urinate so much?"

"Will you stop it?" I said, gritting my teeth.

I stormed to the bathroom, but still she called out,"It's your fourth time urinating today, Freddie! Or are you defecating?"

I went to the bathroom and returned to find an obese, bearded man with food all over his shirt sitting with my mother.

"Freddie, this man is a doctor. Maybe you could talk to him."

That's when I lost it. I cursed and stormed out. A bit later, she met me outside.

"I don't wanna talk to a doctor, I'm fine, goddamn it!" I screamed.

"You're so fresh! You resent me so much. The man was being nice and you didn't want to see him. You'll be happy when I'm gone, Freddie!"

The lesson learned here was at least when you're alone, no one pays attention to how much you go to the bathroom—well, if they do, at least usually they don't say anything to you about it.

Many dates, at least most of mine, were also worse than eating alone. It's hard to pick my most horrific date. I thought it was just last week, when I met this woman for what I thought was a casual brunch. It was one of those Facebook things. Our names came up; we knew each other peripherally from the past. We made Internet small talk and decided to meet up for a brunch at The Daily Milk on Beverly Boulevard. When I got there she started to cry—real tears—when she saw I hadn't shaved. "You don't take me seriously enough to shave for?" People started looking at us so I made an escape to the bathroom. Luckily, she left when she got a phone call for, what she flat-out told me, was a better offer.

But since that date ended rather quickly, I'll refer back to a blind date I had a few months earlier as my worst blind date. I bumped into a friend at a supermarket checkout who asked if I was single, saying he had a great woman for me. I Googled her and was pleasantly surprised by the images I found. She showed up looking like her photos, very attractive, and with a nice, sweet smile. Not even four minutes into our lunch she told me she had a boyfriend.

"Then why'd you come on this blind date?" I asked.

"I looked you up on the IMDb, saw you had some okay credits, and figured it'd be good to have some showbiz contacts," she said. "I could certainly use the help."

Before I tried explaining that I didn't think I could help her career, she whipped out a spec script for *Modern Family* and insisted she act it out for me. I tried to tell her to stop, but she ended up acting out the whole episode as I sat there with my head down. At the end, she asked what I thought.

"I'm sorry, I'm not familiar with *Modern Family*."

She rolled her eyes. "Then why'd you have me read it?"

37

MY AWESOME SHOWBIZ PERKS

One of the perks of being a writer on *Seinfeld* was that I was forced to join the Writers Guild for $1,200. Around this time, I got a phone call from Gary, a guy I'd taken a Learning Annex class with a few years earlier

"You know, Writers Guild members are entitled to three months of free movies. And you can take a guest. Can we go see some movies?"

I was thrilled to have this movie buddy. Seeing a movie alone poses many of the same headaches as eating alone. Weekends and holiday nights are too depressing. Afternoon matinees are good and they're less crowded and less expensive. But I find Monday and Tuesday nights are preferable when the movie warrants a full-price ticket.

I admit, sometimes I have hovered around the lobby at The Grove movie theater in my neighborhood, looking at my watch and pretending to be a normal person waiting for a friend to go see a movie with. It's similar to how I feel when I sit and people-watch next door at The Farmers Market; if I sit on a bench staring into space, I'm a lunatic, but if I have a latte in my hand, I'm a regular person.

So when I feel really cooped up and isolated, sometimes I will just go to the movie theater lobby and hang out for a bit, posing as if I'm waiting for that friend, but really I'm waiting to see if I bump into anyone I know. Don't judge me (probably way too late for that), but the hope is that someone I know will be on their way to see a movie and say, "Hey, come see it with us!" This has never happened. I've only run into annoying people coming out of films who want to tell me everything that just happened in the film; or once, an annoying guy cornered me, telling me racist jokes with garlic breath and saying, "What's with you comedians, you never laugh!"

I'm actually okay sitting alone in the theater—I don't particularly need someone I know sitting next to me and annoying me because they talk too much, or asking questions about something that can only be known by the writer or a psychic, or trying to show how smart they are by pointing to something obvious on the screen. "That's New York City!" But I don't like the part when it's all over and I have no one to talk to about what I just saw. That's kinda the beauty of any movie—it could be the worst piece of garbage ever, but it's worth every cent when you and a buddy can bash apart every unrealistic or corny moment in it. Maybe that's why after a seeing a film, or even a TV show by myself, I like to check out the comments on the IMDB board. It sort of makes me feel like I'm part of a conversation.

I once saw *Dead Man Walking* on a Monday night. There might have been just a dozen people in the whole theater. As I walked out by myself, I lagged behind a group of two couples who were intently discussing the film. I overheard that they were getting a late-night snack at IHOP, and I seriously considered going and trying to get a table by them so I could continue eavesdropping and keep the experience of the film going just a little bit longer. (Elevators are good for this after the movie—you can hear viewers talking about it. But you'd have to do several trips up and down to keep the experience going, and that's even too pathetic for me.)

I wouldn't have known about these free movies with my union card if Gary hadn't alerted me to it, so I figured I'd take him with me. Not only did I have someone to see almost every movie with, but as I wished, our movie viewing usually continued at some restaurant afterward, where we'd discuss the film we had just seen. Gary had a lot of time off like I did. He had sold some family car-detailing business handed down to him while trying to find his way in show business. Except for a few classes, his ability to describe himself as "in showbiz" was akin to me thinking I was a ladies' man. I soon discovered it was very important to Gary to try to seem important, so anywhere we'd go, if he bumped into someone he knew he'd always tell them he was taking lots of meetings. What that meant was that he had business cards made up that said "Producer" on them.

He'd come by to pick me up in his big Jeep. At first I was embarrassed getting into this big, ridiculous, unnecessarily flashy car, but a few moments into our trip to the theater, I'd get over it and feel good that I had a place to go and someone to go there with. And it was free!

I probably went to more movies in that three-month span than in my whole life. And if we got a bite before or after at one of those trendy places with all the couples, it didn't bother me. On a few occasions, Gary even initiated small talk with some women at another table. Nothing came from our little chitchats, but I felt great that I was in the game. I was out and not hiding.

I never entertained the concept that Gary was using me for the free movies. The way I looked at it, it didn't cost me a cent and I liked the company. Well, that's the way I looked at it for most of the three months, but toward the end, some stuff started happening.

I called Gary once to see if he just wanted to grab a bite to eat. We had seen all the movies at our free theater that week.

"Where were you thinking of getting a bite at?" he asked. I suggested this Chinese restaurant I liked. "There's never any chicks around there," he said. I rattled off a few other restaurants and with each one he took a long pause pondering if these were good choices where chicks might possibly be adjacent to our table. And then I started wondering why it wasn't enough to just have a bite with me somewhere, just to do that? Why did there have to be an agenda along with that lunch?

And then I'd hear about parties or bars he'd go to with his slick friends, Brad and Steve. When I asked why I wasn't invited, he told me he liked hanging out with them because they brought his game up with the chicks. Apparently, I wasn't an asset to his social life.

He'd go out of town on surfing and skiing trips with some of those other guys while I watched his house and his cat. That's what friends do, right? And I liked his cat. Maybe he figured I wasn't a surfer, and I wasn't. But I still felt left out.

As soon as the three months were up and free movie season was over, Gary became too busy to see me. He said things were really cooking in the producer business. I'd call to see if he wanted to grab a bite and he'd explain he was staying in and buckling down and getting serious, whatever that meant.

Other people have tried to take advantage of my free movie season too. One woman I was interested in asked if she could borrow my Guild card so she could take dates to free movies. Another friend asked if he could go with his wife. There are about five others who call like clockwork every November when free movie season begins. "Hey Fred! I'm looking in the paper, there's a bunch of movies that look good . . . you're still in the Guild, right?"

But the person who abused this movie privilege the most was myself. I put pressure on myself that I had to see every free film I could. If I had a cold or something else I should have been doing, I still felt I had to see a movie. And some were movies I knew I wouldn't even like, like *Sense and Sensibility*. But hey, it was free.

I made a list every year of all the movies I saw and took other people to, and I admit that I loved looking at the list, adding up how much it would have cost if I'd actually bought a ticket for all these movies and feeling good about how I hadn't.

And then I got very altruistic about it. I'd do my usual lurking outside the movie theater, hoping to bump into someone I knew so I could offer to take them in for free. If that didn't happen and it was nearing show time, I'd scope out someone waiting in line who didn't look like a yuppie.

"Hey, I can get you in for free," I said.

Sometimes they looked very scared and said, "No thanks." I once worked up the nerve to approach a cute girl. She took me up on the free ticket but then sat a few rows behind me.

For ten years I got free movies, and then my Guild membership was due to expire because I had been acting far more than writing. I began to panic that the power of free movies would end; I'd have to be like a normal person and wait in line and actually buy a ticket. What was I going to do without the reign of power?

But when my membership was up, I felt oddly at peace. I realized how much pressure I'd been under to see the movies and then strategically try to take a guest. Now, I thought, people might possibly like me for me and not because I could take them to free movies.

Later, a script I wrote got me back in the Guild. I haven't told anyone until just now.

38

AM I SOMEBODY YET?

I was standing on line to start a new unemployment claim when I got recognized. I humbly shrugged my shoulders and commented something like, "It's no big deal. Look where I am."

"Can I ask you something?" my amazed fan asked. "What do you think was your big break? When did you know you had arrived?"

Was this guy serious? But I could tell by the look on his face, he was. He looked at me transfixed, smiling, laughing to himself, shrugging his shoulders in awe as if he were recalling some of his favorite appearances. My big break? I can't really say. Maybe it was many years later when the unemployment insurance office implemented a system where you could file your claims over the phone insuring the ultimate comfort and anonymity.

There have actually been various validations that have come in unexpected dribs and drabs where I'm able to stand back and go, "Wow! There may actually be something here." Perhaps it was the times I've been on *TMZ*, as the "celebrity" Harvey's sidekicks were trying to figure out just who I was. They all threw in their two cents trying to figure out my name till one of them, looking at his computer, said, "Fred Stoller! That's who he is!" After that I was on several other times as that guy you know, but are never sure where from.

But I'd have to say another example of a confusing achievement came from a simple radio voice-over role. I was actually beating myself up for even reading for this part. It was for British Airways. When you audition for a radio ad, you go in a booth at your agency and they record you. Radio ads are pretty competitive. The agency that represents you also submits, along with your recording, about twenty of their other clients. And about ten other agencies do the same so you figure you're competing with over 200 others for that role.

With all voice-over auditions, along with the lines you're reading you're handed a description of how they envision the character to sound. The character description for this part: "Nervous sort of guy, after all, he's in therapy. Example: Fred Stoller."

It was very surreal seeing my name as a character description. On the one hand it was flattering, but what it really was saying was, "Yeah, you're a unique distinctive guy, but wait at the end of the line with everyone else, you schmuck."

I was already in the booth. It still felt weird. I wish I had more time to think about this. Do I really want to audition for a Fred Stoller type? I was reading with a partner and she was in no mood for my neurosis. She was in a rush and wanted to get the audition over with, so I auditioned to play myself. When you do a voice-over audition, first you have to state your name and character. That means you say your name and your character before you go into the reading. I felt so stupid saying, "Fred Stoller as guy."

I didn't get the part. I was turned down for a Fred Stoller part. Someone at the ad agency listened to my audition and said, "No, this isn't what we want." Maybe when I auditioned I should have said, "Yeah, this is Fred Stoller reading for the Fred Stoller part."

I figured that perfectly summed up my career at that point; it was my proudest moment of humiliation. I was flattered and then smacked in the face at the same time.

39

A ROOMFUL OF WEIRDOS

I recently auditioned for an NBC pilot that was chockful of every kind of weirdo character you could find. I got off the elevator and before I could look around to see which character actors I knew in this massive waiting room, I heard the voice of a pre-teen boy exclaim, "Cool, you were in *Joe Dirt*!

I just had five lines in that movie, but obviously the kid had seen the film dozens of times. I was trying to concentrate on my material as the kid recited every line of his favorite film. His dad, who he tagged along with, was auditioning for the same part as I was, and he eventually told him to let me look my material over too. I smiled knowing I made his day, though the room was spilling with millionaires from previous hit shows looking for their next gig. The kid made my day too.

I looked around and it hammered home this illusion of the steady showbiz home I seek. Next to me was the guy who spent seven years on *According to Jim*, someone who was a regular on *Becker*, *3rd Rock from the Sun*, *Night Court*, *NewsRadio, Spin City, The Sopranos* and many other very familiar actors. I realized all of us were the same—some perhaps had bigger homes with a pool somewhere—but at that moment we were all sitting in the same crammed waiting room. Unless you're Kevin James or Will Smith, you end up back in a room waiting to read for the next role. But I took comfort in that I had succeeded to this point and that I could leave that room if I so chose or I could pick which rooms I wanted to go to. Plus, I was in *Joe Dirt* among many other cool little things.

40

BEING A LEADING MAN

Several years ago, I was on a hot soundstage in Atlanta on the set of *The Change-Up,* playing a production assistant in a movie within a movie. My character was one of a group of frantic crew people getting Ryan Reynolds' character ready for his scene in a soft-core porno shoot. When I got to the set, I found all my lines were cut for some reason. So I ad-libbed "Here" as I shoved a machine gun in Reynolds' stomach as he passed. After our tenth take, the director gave us a note.

"Fred, no talking! Okay, let's do it again without Fred talking! Ready . . ."

That experience would be humbling enough on its own. What made it especially deflating was that it put an end to a high I had been on since the night before. I had just flown in from Chicago where a film I wrote and starred in won "Best in Fest" at the Just For Laughs Film Festival. After the screening, we enjoyed an elegant reception and a Q&A where audience members hung on every detail of the making of it and told us how touched they were by it.

For the first time, I had found a project, not as a guest actor or seventh banana, but one where I was the central character.

This time, the creepy blind date, the bouncer, the truck driver, the annoying landlord, the crazy waiter, all the weird oddball parts, were played by others. It was the story about my friendship with Vinnie D'Angelo, in a screenplay that I wrote called *Fred & Vinnie.*

Joel may have lived vicariously through my free food, but Vinnie lived vicariously through everything I did. That's because Vinnie hardly ever left his Philadelphia apartment. Well, he'd leave every once in a while. Sometimes he had to. He just didn't like to. I always thought of him as the happiest agoraphobic. He was also the adoring parent I never had. I could always call up Vinnie and count on him to make me feel like my life was so amazing. To him, anything I did during the day was brave and incredible. Let's say I went to the post office. With that alone he'd go crazy.

"Get out! No way, man! You mean in the afternoon?! When it's all crowded and all!?"

"Yup," I said proudly. He made me feel going to any crowded place was such a badass thing to do.

"So tell me about the people. Were they all around you? Like, on what sides of you were they? Were you surrounded on every side?!"

"Well, there were people in front and in back of me. And I guess to both sides of me because the line had to curve round and round."

Then, he'd lose it. "No way, man!" he said it with his nasal Philly accent. So I'd keep going.

"So this woman asked for a book of stamps. The teller asked what kind of stamps she wanted, and the woman said, 'I don't care, any stamps. It doesn't matter.'"

This was too much for Vinnie. He was like a parrot the way he'd copy a phrase, "It doesn't matter! Any stamps! The stamps don't matter! They do not matter!" except that a parrot doesn't copy an expression with any kind of emotion. Vinnie's emotion was sincere. He loved every sound, every syllable of whatever information or expression I would relay to him. He'd just take it in and then immediately scream it back out in different ways.

"Doesn't matter! It does not matt-ter! Any stamps! She didn't care. She didn't care what the stamps were! Woo! I'm screamin'! I'm screamin', man!"

Vinnie would have been happy if my trip to the post office had ended with the woman saying she didn't care what the stamps were, but there was more; and I was feeling good that I was making him feel good.

"Okay, so the teller, this black woman, gave the woman 'any' book of stamps, like she requested. The woman looked at them and said, 'I don't want Malcolm X stamps. Anything but these.'"

With that unexpected topper to the story, Vinnie would explode with laughter, and scream at the top of his lungs, "Ahh! Ahh! Anything but these! No way! She didn't say that! Anything but these! Wooo! Woo!"

I met Vinnie around 1985, when we were both working a comedy club in some suburb of Philadelphia. I'm not sure of Vinnie's whole history, but he did at one time have some sort of outside life. I knew that he briefly held a regular job and also did some theater. After that he was able to get by when the big comedy boom of the eighties hit. He never did more than the Philly local comedy club scene. But at that time, he had enough work doing just weekends and one-nighters around town. Plus, he didn't have many expenses. He lived in a little apartment he called The Cave because it was always dark and cozy and he could sleep for hours on end. He loved every second of staying in and doing nothing. All he ever had to do was go out to some club and do his half-hour set, which mainly consisted of old jokes and prank phone calls he made with a phone he brought on stage. Then he'd head back to his cave.

Then one day, I got a very surprising phone call from Vinnie. He said that he always wanted to give acting a shot. He said that maybe one day he'd come to L.A. to see what it was like. He'd stay with me for a week or so, then crash with some other comics he knew from the old Philly club scene. His plan was to poke around, do some extra work, get a feel for it, see what might happen. Wow, was this the same Vinnie who bragged he could sleep for days and days at a time? Come to L.A. and see about acting? He said, "Just get me on a set." His dream was to cozy up to some big star like Bruce Willis, who would then take him under his wing and give him other jobs. "Just get me on a set," Vinnie said. That's all I had to do. He'd take care of the rest.

I was thrilled. I was looking forward to giving Vinnie a personal tour of all the places I had only been able to tell him about on the phone. I was anxious to show him the bookstore where I once saw people lining up outside waiting for it to open.

"People lining up outside waiting for a bookstore to open?! Un-bee-livable. No way man! No way!"

He wanted to see the video store I had gone to many years ago on Christmas Eve. That day, there was a long line ahead of me and because the store would be closed on Christmas, you could get an extra day of videos for free. I rented some movies and also an adult video. Each person ahead of me got a warm "Best Holiday" wish from the owner. But when I came up to the counter, the owner gave me no "Best Holiday" wish. I guess a person renting porn on Christmas Eve did not deserve one.

Vinnie had to see the place. He wanted to see the Chinese owner who denied me the Christmas wish. I was just a little nervous that he'd see the owner, burst out laughing, and get us into trouble.

And he also wanted to go to the pizza place where this kid who worked there asked me to sign their celebrity wall of fame because he had seen my stand-up act years ago on cable. After I signed the wall, the owners made him paint over it because they had no idea who the hell I was.

He wanted and needed to know every detail about every aspect of my life, and I couldn't wait to show it to him. When I lived in New York City in a little studio apartment, I met my mother once for lunch. At one point she really needed the bathroom. We were right near my place, so I told her she should use the one in my apartment. But she couldn't bear to see how I lived. She just didn't want to know. I actually had to lead her up to the bathroom with her eyes closed like she was blind. For Vinnie, nothing about my life was scary or shameful. Every part of my life mattered so intensely to him, sometimes even more than it did to me. I realized it was perhaps quite insane that he wanted to see these things, but I was counting the days until I'd get the chance to show all of them to him.

When he did come, it wasn't as thrilling as I hoped it would be. He arrived and quickly reverted to his agoraphobic ways. He sulked about how none of his other comic friends would help him or return his calls. And although I was looking forward to having the company, even that turned sour. Vinnie would spend an hour each day hogging my bathroom, blow-drying his hair, for what reason I don't know because he never left my apartment.

Vinnie was also the world's fattest vegetarian. His basic diet consisted of candy and pasta. He would smoke cigarettes on the roof, but otherwise he just stayed in and studied his precious baseball card collection. Despite my offer to help him put together a picture and a résumé, he never made a serious effort to get on a set. After months of sleeping on my floor, Vinnie slowly drove me crazy until I finally found him another place to live.

I had told my friend, Steve, about this episode of my life and years later he said, "Let's make a movie out of this story." He had some money saved from his TV writing career, but neither of us knew anything about making a movie and were at a loss as to how we should begin.

We first hooked up with these five knuckle-headed young guys whose job it was to raise money, but who ended up taking money. I knew I was in trouble when one of them punched a table and exclaimed, "Pictures! I wanna see pictures!"

He then ran outside into someone's backyard and kicked some lawn furniture and flower pots as he continued, "This movie will suffer if we don't have pictures!" That became his thing, punching tables and screaming inane showbiz expressions, most often, "I wanna see pictures!"

They'd argue about casting. At one point, they used valuable money that could've gone to the project to fly to Northern California to audition Steve Wozniak for the role of Vinnie. It was surreal that this billionaire inventor was auditioning to be this weird guy no one knew. If the real Vinnie (who sadly died in 2001) had lived, he'd be cracking up about that. When Steve and I argued that Wozniak wasn't right, these wannabe moguls would exclaim, "We're the producers! You back off and let us do what we do 'cause we're producers!"

"He's not an actor. You saw that from his audition," I said.

"He has a following!"

"So do Tony Hawk and Curtis Sliwa from The Guardian Angels," I tried reasoning.

The knuckleheads did, however, introduce us to a great and resourceful line producer who pulled all the elements together for us. Before we knew it, sets were built and trucks full of equipment were being unloaded by hard-working crew guys wearing bandannas and tattoos. We shot the whole thing in nineteen days.

With *Fred & Vinnie*, I finally got first billing, not that that was ever a craving eating me alive my whole career . . . And working on the set, I tried my best to imitate those stars, the humble ones, the thoughtful ones, who over the course of my twenty years of guest appearances made me feel welcome and important. Basically I thanked people a lot, and made sure they knew what great food there was at the craft service table. I was very supportive and nice during the auditions and even pushed for many parts to be cast without the actor having to come in and read if I felt it wasn't necessary. And for nineteen extraordinary days, my cast and crew and I shared quite a happy home.

After post-production, we entered and were accepted into a bunch of film festivals: Slamdance, Newport Beach, Austin, and Just For Laughs in both Chicago and Montreal, to name a few. I even won a best actor award at the Mammoth Film Festival. At the Austin Film Festival we won the audience award in the Comedy Vanguard category. Eventually, we landed with a small distributor who made our little movie available on video on demand.

During our festival run, I was surprised to find out we had even been asked to screen as part of a mental health program. The program director was sure it would fit in splendidly with their documentaries about mental disorders. That gave me pause. I was always a little dumbfounded when someone would describe *Fred & Vinnie* as a film about two pathetic people because basically I was playing myself. It made me think about how I presented myself to the outside world. Sure, I was on the fringes of show business, but I didn't have a suffocating job with a ball-breaking boss. I wasn't in debt. I'd go days without even having to set my alarm clock, let alone be trapped in rush hour traffic ten times a week. True, my apartment wasn't one you'd see on *Cribs* or *Celebrity Homes*, but my rent was always paid on time with the showbiz jobs I had. Okay, my character *was* compiling a list of all the restaurants *he* didn't feel self-conscious eating alone at, and he couldn't wait for his agoraphobic friend to see where he bought videos tapes to validate his life. Okay, maybe some of those things might have been autobiographical . . . but the reactions to the film made me realize that I was actually, if not "happy" with my life, at least content with how it all had turned out. I wasn't pathetic at all. I liked my life. I had a career and I had friends. So many of the people I had started with in New York and L.A. had since been either forced out of the business or given up to do other things. But I had beaten the odds.

41

HOME

Last year, I was visiting my parents at their retirement community in Florida. This time it actually hadn't been all that hellacious. My parents were thrilled when, at a Chinese restaurant, a fourteen-year-old kid approached me and asked for my autograph. He was a fan of *Raymond*, which was now very big in syndication. My mother kept repeating how mind "bottling" it was that he asked for my autograph.

After that, my mother introduced me to some of her neighbors as her "son that's been on TV." I was a bit shocked when she told me why she introduced me that way. I heard her say words I had never heard her say before: she was proud of me. I felt after so many years I was begrudgingly tolerated by her. I never thought I was enough. I thought I was her weirdo son who walks the streets aimlessly like a mental patient during the day. All my work never seemed to add up to the big payoff.

But maybe I was wrong. Maybe I saw myself that way in the past. She actually said she was proud of me and I really felt it. She may have in fact have said those words before. If she had, I never could discern them through all her other comments I had interpreted as negative and all-encompassing.

Yes, she was proud of what I had achieved, but still kept asking me if any other work for me was coming up. Nothing was, but I guess she figured that her persistent badgering would somehow force an upcoming week of employment. But something had changed. I was more patient. I answered all of her same questions over and over and over.

I had devised a strategy for my visit after my last one ended with me being chided. I had thought I was being patient. I didn't blow up at her or tell her to stop bugging me about how much money I'm making or why I'm not further along. But I suppose sitting there grimacing in pain, answering her questions with as few syllables as possible, came off like I was a prisoner of war with nothing but the thought of liberation keeping me alive.

I realized we were all aging and there might not be too many of these trips left. I decided I wasn't going to again break out in a stress rash, pleading for Valium after my search of their medicine cabinet came up empty. I wasn't going to be miserable. I was hoping that by being as upbeat as I could and by acting in no way that could be minutely misconstrued as resentful, I wouldn't be making them miserable either.

This trip my mother wouldn't be able to accuse me of just shortly answering her questions about my life and career. I would actually initiate conversation. I'd talk about my life and all that I enjoyed. In the past I had just brushed off questions about what I did during the day like I was ashamed of myself. But I had no shame. I excitedly described every detail. I explained how yes, I don't really work at one steady place, but how exciting it is that at any supermarket or mall, there's always the possibility I could bump into someone I have worked with on one of my many TV visits. I could encounter a prop master, fellow actor, grip, or any number of crew members I have worked with and that makes me feel not so alone.

I explained what these various showbiz crew people I sometimes bump into do. They were actually excited to hear what goes into the making of a TV show and some of my stories about the sets I've worked on. I told them how exciting it is to be sort of like a detective, always going on any lead I can. I admitted some days I don't know what the hell to do with myself, but it all works out eventually. Just talking about it, not shunning it, made us all less shameful about myself.

I explained why I felt it's hard to meet that special woman and how I don't wish to just settle. I didn't lie and make up my usual fake girlfriend to avoid their, and possibly my own, pity. And there was no pity. I felt the most accepted when my mother said, "Not everyone's meant to be married."

My strategy worked. It wasn't like a movie where we broke down crying as we hugged and exclaimed how we loved each other. We didn't have to. Just the fact that my visit wasn't that torturous was one of my most surprising successes ever. I was actually anxious to return again to see if my exciting new achievement in tolerance wasn't just a fluke. I was looking forward to calling more than I usually did to keep them posted about further developments of any kind. It was a good trip, but of course, I still was so happy to be coming home to L.A.

I looked out the airplane window and thought about my apartment. I couldn't wait to see my cats and see what mail had piled up. I couldn't wait to return to The Grove. Just several years earlier, there was a big vacant lot near my apartment. Before The Grove, I used to have to walk a mile to the Beverly Center Mall just to eat at the food court, look through the bookstore, and feel I was interacting. The Grove is not so much a mall, but more like a movie set of a fake town where I consider myself the self-anointed mayor. There is a trolley that passes through the two-block village and the operator waves to me when he passes by. There are not only stores, but little kiosks outside the shops. The man who runs the Sunglass Hut shakes my hand when he sees me and wants to take a photo of me wearing a pair of his sunglasses. I have a VIP card that entitles me to free desserts at the restaurants. I'm the one that the struggling actors who work at the retail stores know as the guy that's been on TV. They ask me for advice. Some have even offered to quit their jobs to be my assistant. I explain that I can't afford an assistant and there wouldn't be much for them to do than perhaps meander about with me. Their view of me is flattering and as surreal to me as when I auditioned for the "Fred Stoller" part and didn't get it.

As the plane touched down, I started to feel the same excitement I had when I first landed at Los Angeles airport in 1988. Back then, I was relocating to a new world of possibilities. I thought anything could happen. I wasn't thinking about all the politics and the immeasurable odds. The plane came to a stop and I stepped out, feeling excited, not thinking about all my past heartache and assorted defeats. Maybe this feeling wouldn't last. But, for now, I was home. And everything was all ahead for me.

Acknowledgments

To David Handleman, a smart guy who liked the idea when we met for generously spending a lot of time giving me his very useful take.

To Steve Skrovan who also helped a lot, not to mention he was there for so much of this little journey.

To Joel Warshawer, another friend, and big part of the story who still roots for me to get work so he can hear what free food I get.

To Patrick Downing and Justin Roiland. Thanks for lighting the fire in me to keep pushing this.

To the ones who have "had me back" on their shows: Phil Rosenthal, Tom Palmer, Steve Peterman, Gary Dontzig, Mike Saltzman, Dan Yaccarino, Fran Drescher, Ray Romano, Tom Snyder, Loren Bouchard, Jonathan Katz, Norman Steinberg, Todd J. Greenwald, Meredith Layne, Dorothea Gillim.

Thanks to George Calfa. If it weren't for your tech support, most of these words written a long time ago wouldn't be saved.

Thanks to Cari Lynn for her help, and introducing me to my wonderful agent, Jill Marr.

To my editor Marianna Dworak and everyone at Skyhorse Publishing for wanting to do this book.

To these people who've helped, or been great friends: Robert Cabeen, John Over, Jeff Mandell, Rob Bartlett, Chris Rock, Bob Saget, Sarah Silverman, Fred and Mary Willard, Howie Mandel, Angelo Tsarouchas, Eric Wilkinson, David Blum, Jerry Magana, Beth Gardiner, Aaron Moles, Louanne Johnson, Treat Williams, Heath Hyche, Brad Garrett, Nancy Kanter, and Robyn Ginsburg Hardy.

To anyone I've left out who I've used the word "mensch" to describe. But why do you guys have to be so rare?

And to everyone who ever said to me, "Hey, I know you," "You're funny," "Keep it up!" You guys always make my day.